PRAISE FOR SI

"Rev. Daniel London has captured the essential content of St. Aelred's famous, twelfth-century treatise on spiritual friendship and enhanced its dialogic form, giving it an updated expression. The result is a readable, inspirational text suitable to be read aloud at a parish gathering or retreat as a spur for an extended conversation about friendship as a special form of human and divine love. Dedicated to the memory of two of his own friends, London's *Spiritual Friendship, Distilled* awakens longing and gratitude for the gift of true friendship it describes and defines."

—Ann W. Astell, Professor of Theology, University of Notre Dame

"*Spiritual Friendship, Distilled* is an invitation to free yourself from the crowd, learn how to embody the transformative beauty of spiritual friendship, and dip the world in the sweet honey of divine love. This adaptable book will be helpful in academic classrooms, on spiritual retreats, during zoom conversations among friends, and even performed at local theaters. Here, friend, I trust you will find medicine for the global loneliness epidemic wounding our hearts and alienating us from each other."

—Paul Houston Blankenship-Lai, Assistant Professor of Spirituality, Earlham School of Religion

"A remarkable meditation on the deepest stratum of friendships. This book led me on a journey of reflection about my choices in friends, what agreements—often unspoken—existed between us, and how the bonds we shared have supported each other's lives. There are many threads in this book that equip us to become better friends and spiritual companions."

—Amos Clifford, founder of the Association of Nature and Forest Therapy and author of *Your Guide to Forest Bathing*.

"The Rev Dr Daniel London writes with deep insight into the matters of spirituality. He brings a remarkable combination of strengths: a wholehearted love of God, theological depth, and a broad engagement with the community around him. Further, the work is grounded in the realities of caring for his own congregation in the midst of a changing, post-pandemic world. If you come across his books—read them!"

—Bishop Megan Traquair, Episcopal Diocese of Northern California

---

"Aelred's insights about friendship remain as fresh and relevant as they were during the twelfth-century monastic renewal he helped lead. This distillation is much more than a summary: it makes his words leap across the centuries and speak with a contemporary voice while keeping the conversational format and feel of Aelred's treatise. By condensing the fuller discussions in the Latin original, it clarifies the main threads that weave through the three dialogues. A concise introduction gives a glimpse into the various cultural traditions of friendship—Celtic Christian, Anglo-Saxon, classical, and monastic—that Aelred inherited and synthesized. Brief notes indicate his sources and also suggest connections to more recent thinkers about friendship such as C. S. Lewis. As a bonus, three beautiful, Aelred-inspired practices at the end connect spiritual friendship to Buddhist meditation and forest therapy."

—Curtis Gruenler, Professor of English, Hope College

"This little book radiates with Love and Friendship. First, Daniel brings us into the heart of Aelred of Rievaulx's writings. And then, he goes beyond Aelred, offering us simple meditation practices that have the potential to expand our hearts in friendship with self, other, and the Divine. If you wish to deepen your friendships, run to bring these words to your heart."

—Alexander John Shaia, author and teacher at www.quadratos.org

SPIRITUAL FRIENDSHIP, DISTILLED

ST. AELRED OF RIEVAULX

DISTILLED BY
THE REV. DANIEL DEFOREST LONDON, PHD

APOCRYPHILE
PRESS

Apocryphile Press
PO Box 255
Hannacroix, NY 12087
www.apocryphilepress.com

Copyright © 2024 by Daniel DeForest London
Printed in the United States of America
ISBN 978-1-958061-84-8 | paper
ISBN 978-1-958061-78-7 | ePub

Cover painting by David Giles Lochtie.

Please join our mailing list at www.apocryphilepress.com/free. We'll keep you up-to-date on all our new releases, and we'll also send you a FREE BOOK. Visit us today!

CONTENTS

FOREWORD

SIMEON LEIVA-MERIKAKIS, OCSO

Ælred of Rievaulx's treatise *On Spiritual Friendship* is a jewel of monastic Christian literature. This medieval classic is itself already a distillation of the wisdom of Antiquity, with deep roots in Cicero, Aristotle and even the *Iliad* and the *Epic of Gilgamesh*. St Ælred, a 12th-century English Cistercian monk and a beloved disciple of Bernard of Clairvaux, exhibits with great verve the universality of the human need for friendship as transfigured by the Gospel of Christ, in particular the mystical strain of Johannine affectivity.

Although I was at first a little skeptical about the whole notion of "distilling" great works of the spiritual life, I have been won over by Daniel London's sterling achievement in *Spiritual Friendship, Distilled*. Everything depends upon the quality of the "distillation". The crucial question is: How authentically does this approach succeed in conveying, in greatly abbreviated form and in contemporary idiom, the integrity of the original's scope and impact? London's generous introduction and scholarly endnotes reassure the reader that the author knows his material thoroughly and can, therefore, be trusted with the judgments he makes in producing the text before us.

The power of the results speaks for itself. London's evident authorial wisdom, at once scholarly and pastoral, beautifully illustrates the difference between mere "abridgment" and true *distillation*. Just as lemon zest contains the essence of the lemon tree and honey the essence of the hive, this book communicates in highly attractive form the essence of Ælred's dialog on friendship, shorn of rhetorical flourishes and complex allegories.

Daniel London's *Spiritual Friendship, Distilled* will serve well both the spirit-quester, short on reading time yet avid for solid nourishment, and the more leisurely depth-diver, who will be baited by this book to plumb the sweet fullness and fire of Ælred's thought in the original.

Simeon Leiva-Merikakis, OCSO
St Joseph's Cistercian Abbey
Spencer, MA

Dedicated to

Jacob Rodgers Pierce (1983–2023)
&
Daniel Torkelson Strenge (1983–2014)

Spiritual friends who remain alive in my heart

One Love
Eternal Love

INTRODUCTION

"I do not call you servants...
but I have called you friends."
—John 15:15

The original patron saint of friendship is St. John the Apostle and Evangelist, who, according to tradition, was the beloved disciple who reclined upon the bosom of his rabbi, listening to the heartbeat of the teacher who also became his friend.[1] The association between friendship, the heart, and the beloved disciple persisted and peaked among the eighth-century Celtic Christians, who portrayed the evangelist in their Lindisfarne Gospels holding his right hand over his heart.[2] According to John's Gospel, Jesus called his disciples "friends" because he shared with them the secrets of his heart.[3] The Celtic understanding of John suggests that our friendships with each other and the divine can deepen whenever we access and activate the "heart sense" simply by placing our hand on our chest.

Saint Cuthbert (634–687), the beloved bishop of Lindisfarne, was buried with a copy of St. John's Gospel resting on his heart, a book that he read prayerfully with a spiritual friend and prophet named Boisil, days before Boisil passed away.[4] St. Cuthbert was buried in a coffin that included an oak carving of St. John once again holding his right hand over his chest. The care and protection of this treasured coffin later fell to a sacristan named Alfred, the great grandfather of an English Cistercian monk and abbot whose life and teachings invite us to connect with the heart of friendship and the friendship of the heart, especially through his classic text titled *Spiritual Friendship*.

Like a river fed by many streams, the medieval author of *Spiritual Friendship* was fed and informed by several streams of spiritual thought about friendship. Born in England, raised in Scotland, and commissioned by a French Cistercian abbot to write treatises in Latin, St. Aelred of Rievaulx (1110–1167) integrated not only Celtic Christianity, but also Anglo-Saxon spirituality, Roman Classic philosophy, and Cistercian spirituality. His treatise on *Spiritual Friendship* subtly weaves together the wisdom of the Celtic "soul friend," the fierce loyalty of the Anglo-Saxon *comitatus*, the eloquence of Cicero, and the mystical love of St. Bernard of Clairvaux. Carrying on the legacy of the evangelist, Aelred's thoughtful integration and heartfelt invitations have earned him the right to not only share with St. John the appellation "patron saint of friendship" but to also be honored as the classic Christian expert on the subject. Anyone interested in friendship from a spiritual perspective, or in spiritual growth in general, would be wise to read, mark, learn, and inwardly digest Aelred's *Spiritual Friendship*.

The threefold intent of this distilled version of *Spiritual Friendship* is to share Aelred's wisdom with a wider audience, to pique people's interest in reading the original text (even in

Latin),[5] and to invite those who are already familiar with the text to hear it in a new and refreshing way. In this introduction and distillation, I hope to shed some light on how Aelred, to borrow a phrase from Cicero, made "one out of many" by creating a sophisticated and nuanced spirituality of friendship out of the many philosophies and theologies of friendship that formed him.

AELRED AND ANAMCARA: CELTIC SOUL FRIENDS

> *"A person without a soul friend*
> *is like a body without a head."*
> —St. Brigid of Kildare[6]

With spiritual roots in the Gospel of John, the Celtic Christian tradition emphasized the importance of a friend who can accompany us along our life journey, a friend whom the ancient Celts called an *anamcara*. The term *anamcara*, which is Gaelic for "soul friend," has enjoyed renewed popularity ever since the Irish poet John O'Donohue published his influential book *Anam Cara: Spiritual Wisdom from the Celtic World*, in which he defines the soul friend as "someone to whom you confessed, revealing the hidden intimacies of your life. With the *anam cara* you could share your innermost self, your mind, and *your heart.*"[7] O'Donohue's poetic reflections on the concept of the Celtic soul friend helped inspire the publication of a plethora of books on Celtic spirituality and soul friendship along with the formation of a religious community called the Anamchara Fellowship.[8] One of O'Donohue's more powerful conclusions is inspired by Aelred himself: "Friendship," according to O'Donohue, "is the nature of God. The Christian concept of God as Trinity is the most sublime articulation of Otherness and intimacy, an eternal interflow of friendship."[9] In Book I of Aelred's treatise, his friend and interlocutor Ivo suggests more succinctly, "God is Friendship," a proposition upon which Aelred proceeds to elaborate with poetic insight.

Although much of O'Donohue's musings might be considered more pop psychology than ancient Celtic wisdom, there is indeed evidence of an early Celtic emphasis on spiritual friendship, as seen in the writings of John Cassian, who carried the wisdom of the desert fathers and mothers to the Celtic monks in a fifth-century text titled *Conferences*. In his *Conferences*, Cassian describes friendship as an indestructible bond between two virtuous individuals committed to seeking the good, a description that resonates well with the definition developed by Aelred, who was, no doubt, familiar with the *Conferences*.[10] Also, there is an ancient account of St. Brigid of Kildare speaking to a young priest whose friend had recently died. As the daughter of both a druid and a Christian, Brigid may have been integrating pre-Christian Celtic wisdom about friendship when she expressed sympathy for the cleric, saying, "a person without a soul friend is like a body without a head," followed by advice for the priest to fast and pray until God brought him a new spiritual companion.[11] Aelred, who insisted that no one can be happy without friends, would likely agree with Brigid's prescription.

Although born in Northumbria, the Celtic Christian stream and its *anamcara* current flowed mightily in Aelred's ancestry. His great grandfather Alfred served as the guardian and treasurer of the tomb of St. Cuthbert of Lindisfarne (d. 687), successor to the Irish missionary monk St. Aidan, who was trained on the island of Iona, the central hub of Celtic Christian missions to the northern British Isles.[12] At the age of 14, young Aelred served in the court of King David of Scotland, so throughout his teenage years and early twenties, Aelred was immersed in the upper-class world of Christian Scotland and was thus soaked in the atmosphere of ancient and medieval Celtic spirituality. It was during this time that Aelred was given a book from his friend and teacher Lawrence of Durham titled *The Life of Saint Brigid of Kildare*, a hagiography of the same Celtic saint who insisted that an *anamcara* was just as necessary for our survival as our head.[13] *The Life of Saint Brigid* recounts the female saint's magnanimous friendships with dogs, ducks, bishops, nuns, priests, and most of all, the poor. In *Spiritual Friendship*, Aelred explains that one of the best ways to discern whether a friend has good intentions is to notice how they treat the poor, an insight that may have likely been inspired by St. Brigid's charitable generosity.

The influence of the Celtic concept of *anamcara* remains subtle and implicit in Aelred's *Spiritual Friendship*, but it is not hard to imagine the integration of Celtic Christian spirituality in his writings, not only because he lived in Scotland and read *The Life of Saint Brigid*, but also because his ancestors were caretakers of the tomb of St. Cuthbert, who represents the affable balance and integration of the Celtic and Anglo-Saxon worlds.

AELRED THE ANGLO-SAXON: FIERCELY LOYAL OPPOSITION

> *"A young prince must be prepared*
> *with loyal companions."*
> —an Anglo-Saxon maxim[14]

In his book *English Spirituality*, Anglican priest and author Martin Thornton describes the English spiritual tradition, which he calls the "English School," as characterized by a friendly and almost familial bond across social class and political status.[15] With this bond, friends are not afraid to challenge each other, even if one of the friends might be in a position of authority over the other. Thornton writes, "Our distrust of clericalism and authoritarianism is no shallow—or modern—trait, but the result of a long pastoral heritage, based on the doctrine of the Body of Christ."[16] This long pastoral heritage may be traced all the way back to the Anglo-Saxon *witan,* which was an assembly of noblemen who advised the king. The English propensity to advise, question, and even challenge authority may have contributed to the development of the English parliament, the signing of the Magna Carta, the constitutional monarchy, and perhaps even the Church of England's rejection of the pope's authority in the sixteenth century. At its best, this questioning of authority is not driven by rebellious and destructive forces, but rather by constructive and responsible loyalty. In Anglo-Saxon poems like *Beowulf* and *The Dream of the Rood,* we see expressions of fierce loyalty, especially between the king and his thanes who comprised a group known as *comitatus.* The warrior or thane within the *comitatus* would be bound by loyal allegiance to fight in a battle and even die for the king, who in turn would provide support, honor, and reward. The devoted allegiance of the *comitatus* is implied in the Anglo-Saxon proverb: "A young prince must be prepared with loyal companions."[17]

Aelred, who was born in Hexham Northumbria and who came from a long line of Anglo-Saxon priests, developed a close friendship with King David's son, Prince Henry, thus helping him fulfill part of an ideal prince's obligation to be "be prepared with loyal companions."[18] Aelred's Anglo-Saxon blood and early upbringing may have contributed not only to his fierce loyalty to Prince Henry and King David but also to his audacity in offering constructive advice. Impressed with Aelred's loyal integrity, the king quickly promoted him to head steward of the royal household.

When he later became the abbot of Rievaulx, Aelred occupied a position of authority, vulnerable to other people's questions and challenges. In reading *Spiritual Friendship*, we see how comfortable Aelred's character seems to be in response to the questions, confusions, and critiques of his monastic subordinates and interlocutors Ivo, Walter, and Gratian. He does not seem threatened at all because he trusts in their loyalty. By presenting his ideas in the form of a dialogue with friends who do not always agree, Aelred invites readers today to enter the same conversation authentically with the freedom to disagree within the safety of Aelred's "theological *witan.*" In his first book *Mirror of Charity*, Aelred says, "Let us correct one another, knowing that wounds from a friend are better than an enemy's deceitful kisses."[19] In light of these characteristics of Anglo-Saxon spirituality, we ought not be surprised when we read how much Aelred stresses loyalty as a key quality to seek in a spiritual friend, along with frank honesty.

AELRED THE CICERONIAN: CLASSIC DIPPED IN HONEY

> *"When each person loves the other as much as himself,*
> *it makes one out of many, as Pythagoras*
> *wishes things to be in friendship."*
> —Marcus Tullius Cicero[20]

While the influence of the Celtic *anamcara* and the Anglo-Saxon *comitatus* remain subtle and implicit in Aelred's *Spiritual Friendship*, the impact of Cicero's classic treatise on friendship is anything but subtle. Most of Aelred's insights can be traced back to Cicero's *De Amicitia* (On Friendship), which Aelred explicitly acknowledges as a major influence and inspiration in his preface and throughout his text. Like many classical treatises, Cicero's reflection on friendship is expressed in the form of a dialogue. The primary speaker Laelius shares his wisdom with his two sons-in-law Fannius and Scaevola while sitting on a semi-circular garden bench, which is a particularly Ciceronian setting since, according to the philosopher, "If you have a garden and a library you have everything you need."[21] Laelius reflects on friendship after losing his dear friend Scipio. So, for Cicero, friendship is not a purely abstract concept, but one rooted in real-life experience and, in this case, heart-wrenching loss. The theme of loss appears throughout Aelred's *Spiritual Friendship*, which begins as a dialogue between Aelred and a friend named Ivo who dies between Books I and II.

According to Cicero, friendship is the greatest gift given to humanity by the immortal gods; and friendship, he insists, can only truly exist among individuals seeking to live good and virtuous lives.[22] Cicero emphasizes the importance of loyalty, goodwill, and equality among friends, while also discussing the role of promotions among companions and the process of gradually "unstitching" friendships that need to discontinue, themes clearly echoed by Aelred. A superficial reading of both Cicero's and Aelred's texts might lead one to conclude that Aelred's work is simply a copy of Cicero with a dash of Christian theology and a sprinkling of biblical references. Although Aelred himself describes his work as "Cicero dipped in the sweet honey of Christ's love," the saint deserves more credit than he gives himself. One scholar explains that Aelred "does not limit himself to 'copying' Cicero. He takes Cicero as an inspiration, transforms him, interprets him and, where necessary, completes him with other input. As a result, the philosophical world drawn from Cicero is not diluted in Aelred's text, but rather is renewed, and set, as it were, in the framework of a superior logic."[23]

For instance, while Cicero stresses the importance of loyalty, Aelred highlights three more key qualities to seek in a friend: patience, good intention, and discretion. Aelred then offers his friendly interlocutors advice on how to identify these qualities by reweaving some of the teachings of Cicero. A friend, according to Cicero, ought to be very slow to believe any harmful rumors about their beloved companion; and Aelred uses this kind of sensitive behavior as evidence for a potential friend's discretion.[24] Also, a close reading of *Spiritual Friendship* suggests that each of the four qualities Aelred highlights—loyalty, patience, good intention, and discretion —can be understood as essential virtues for the spiritual journey that will inevitably involve change, suffering, joy, and self-giving service. "Virtue," Cicero claims, "cannot attain her highest aims unattended, but only in union and fellowship with another."[25] Aelred agrees, but his four qualities point to a much more expansive and elaborate understanding of the spiritual path toward those higher aims.[26]

At the same time, Cicero's ageless wisdom ought not be downplayed. He underscores the importance of the heart's role in friendship when he says, "Unless you behold and show an open heart, you can have no loyalty...and not even the satisfaction of loving and being loved, since you do not know what true love is."[27] Decades before Jesus of Nazareth distilled the entire Torah into two commandments—love God and love your neighbor as yourself—Cicero wrote, "When each person loves the other as much as himself, it makes one out of many, as Pythagoras wishes things to be in friendship."[28] While serving as the Presiding Bishop of the Episcopal Church, Michael Curry reminded the USA of the Ciceronian origins of the phrase written on most American currency, *e pluribus unum*: "Cicero, who gave us those words, said that love for each other is the way to make *e pluribus unum* real. Jesus of Nazareth taught us that. Moses taught us that. America, listen to Cicero, Jesus, Moses! Love is the way to make *e pluribus unum* real. Love is the way to *be* America for real."[29] The 2,000-year-old wisdom of Cicero, according to Bishop Curry, remains especially pertinent today in its invitation to open-hearted unity within diversity.

AELRED THE CISTERCIAN: "THE BERNARD OF THE NORTH"

"The more surely you know yourself loved,
the easier you will find it to love in return."
—St. Bernard of Clairvaux[30]

Although Cicero may indeed deserve mention among such august company as Jesus and Moses, Dante unfortunately placed the philosopher in Limbo, a disappointing residency considering the fact that Dante found Cicero's *De Amicitia* especially consoling after the death of his Beatrice. In the same Divine Comedy, Dante's beloved Beatrice could only take him so far as his guide through the spiritual realms. When he reached the highest heaven, he was introduced to his new guide: St. Bernard of Clairvaux. Arguably the most influential church leader of the twelfth century, St. Bernard of Clairvaux (1090–1153) convinced hundreds of men to join the monastery with his eloquence and piety while founding 68 monasteries in the process, including the abbey of Rievaulx. Five hundred years earlier, Pope Gregory the Great had popularized the Rule of St. Benedict among monasteries throughout Western Europe, partly because it was less strict than other monastic rules at the time and proved more accommodating to the humanity of the monks and nuns. For instance, the Rule of St. Benedict humorously states, "We read that monks should not drink wine at all, but since the monks of our day cannot be convinced of this, let us at least agree to drink moderately, and not to the point of excess."[31] Over the centuries, Benedictine monasteries grew exceedingly wealthy, and such opulence made it easier for leaders to ignore some of the stricter aspects of the Rule and to fall into laxity and laziness.[32] So, in the High Middle Ages, reform movements emerged that sought to return to a more faithful adherence to the Rule.[33] None were more successful than the Cistercian movement, spearheaded by St. Bernard.

Known as the last of the Church Fathers, St. Bernard earned the name "Mellifluous Doctor" since his words and wisdom seemed to flow as smoothly and pleasantly as sweet honey, a favorite culinary image that Bernard and Aelred use frequently in their metaphors. About a hundred years before Rumi composed his mystical love poetry, St. Bernard of Clairvaux wrote his sermons on the Song of Songs, significantly deepening and expanding the Christian tradition of erotic mysticism.[34] Understanding the sensual and sexual poetry as an allegorical expression of loving union between God and his people, Bernard offered profound reflections on the mystical "kiss of the mouth" in the Song of Songs, which certainly influenced Aelred's own categories of the holy kiss. While Bernard interpreted the "kiss of the mouth" as the mystical union that follows the previous stages of purgation (the kiss of the feet) and illumination (the kiss of the hand), Aelred delineates between the physical, spiritual, and mystical kiss experienced within the context of friendship.[35]

Also, the degrees of love described in Bernard's *On Loving God* underpin Aelred's teachings on friendship. Bernard suggested that the first stage of love is love of self for the sake of self, followed by a love of God for the sake of self. In other words, after maturing beyond a purely self-centered love, we learn to love God, but still for selfish reasons: hope for eternal life, blessings, etc. The third stage is love of God for God's sake, when we learn to love God not for the sake of any personal benefits we may receive but simply because God is God. And the final stage is love of self for God's sake; that is, a healthy self-love. Aelred, who earned the monikers the "Bernard of the North" as well as the "Doctor of Spiritual Love,"[36] uses the ancient concept of Sabbath to explain similar stages of love for ourselves, our neighbors, and God.[37] By interpreting the Sabbath commandments in the light of Christ's teaching to love God and to love our neighbor as ourselves, Aelred develops what he calls the "Sabbaths of Love." He says, "Let love of self be our first Sabbath, love of neighbor the second, and love of God the Sabbath of Sabbaths."[38] He elaborates on the expanding stages of love for neighbor, which he correlates with the six years preceding the Sabbath year. According to Aelred, we first love our blood relatives (which correlates with year one), then our special friends (year two), then our colleagues and companions (year three), our fellow Christians (year four), non-Christians (year five), enemies (year six). In Aelred's "Sabbaths of Love," there is an ever-widening circle of love that begins with an appropriate self-love. "Truly," Aelred says, "he who does not love his own soul will not be able to love the soul of another."[39]

Appropriate self-love remains central and foundational to

Bernard's understanding of love and Aelred's understanding of friendship. So, what is the impetus for appropriate self-love? What is the reason and motivation for loving the self? According to Cistercian wisdom, we love ourselves not because we are perfect or especially magnificent in our own eyes, but because we believe that God loves us; and God's love for us makes us undeniably and eternally lovable. We are God's craftsmanship, and it would be an insult to God for us to belittle an expression of God's creativity and to deny love for that which God has deemed beloved: ourselves. C. S. Lewis, another expert on the subject of friendship, explained that if God loves us and we refuse to love ourselves then we would essentially be "setting up ourselves as a higher tribunal than Him."[40]

According to Bernard, "The more surely you know yourself loved, the easier you will find it to love in return."[41] So accepting and deepening the experience of our belovedness in God's eyes remains crucial for growing in love and friendship with others. Thomas Merton, the most popular Cistercian author of the twentieth century, echoed Bernard's and Aelred's teaching in his own inspired way when he wrote, "The beginning of the fight against hatred, the basic Christian answer to hatred, is not the commandment to love, but what must necessarily come before in order to make the commandment bearable and comprehensible. It is a prior commandment, *to believe*. The root of Christian love is not the will to love, but *the faith that one is loved*. The faith that one is loved *by God*."[42] With these words, we return to the heart. We return to the image of the beloved disciple leaning upon the bosom of his divine teacher and friend, whose heart beats with goodwill and affection for all those whom God has deemed lovable and whose heart encompasses all spiritual friendships.

THE TEXT AND THE INVITATION

This distillation of *Spiritual Friendship* begins with a distilled version of a letter that Bernard wrote to Aelred in which he commissions him to start writing in the first place. Bernard charges Aelred to write his first major treatise *Mirror of Charity*, which was followed by *Spiritual Friendship*. In the letter, Bernard emphasizes the wisdom expressed through the stones and trees, a theme that appears throughout Aelred's writings and which I sought to highlight throughout the text.[43] For example, in a minor treatise about Jesus as a boy, Aelred writes that whenever we have trouble finding Jesus at traditional holy sites, we should look for him "in the fields and the woods."[44]

The dialogical format of *Spiritual Friendship* invites readers to share the reading experience with others in a friendly "reader's theater" style wherein a *Dramatis Personae* may include Bernard, Ivo, Walter, Gratian, and, of course, Aelred, who has the lion's share of lines. Although the entire text can be read in about an hour, readers may want to pause and reflect after reading Books I and II and perhaps when the cellarer almost interrupts the dialogue in Book III. Along with reading the dialogue with others, the invitation of the distillation is to cultivate a practice of heart-centered prayer for friends, thus deepening our friendship with the divine[45] and nurturing the same goodwill that Aelred expresses in his own *Pastoral Prayer* when he prayed these distilled words for his monks: *May God's gracious providence hold you and sustain you; may God's loving purpose gladden and guide you; and may God's everlasting peace fill you now and always. Amen.*[46]

INTRODUCTION

1. For the Celtic Christian reception of John and the heartbeat of Christ, see John Philip Newell, *Listening for the Heartbeat of God: A Celtic Spirituality* (Mahwah NJ: Paulist Press, 1997). Also, see Daniel DeForest London, "The Sensual Gospel of St. John the Evangelist: A Celtic and Anglican Reception History of the Fourth Gospel," *Anglican Journal of Theology in Aotearao and Oceania* Volume 2, Issue 2, Spring 2023, 6–20.

2. Susan Cremin, "St. John and the bosom of the Lord in Patristic and Insular tradition," in *The Beauty of God's Presence in the Fathers of the Church: The Proceedings of the Eighth International Patristic Conference, Maynooth, 2012,* ed. Janet Elaine Rutherford (Portland OR: Four Courts Press, 2014), 199, 204.

3. John 15:15.

4. The Venerable Bede, *Life of Cuthbert,* Ch 8 in *The Age of Bede*, translated by J. F. Webb (New York: Penguin Books, 1988), 53.

5. I recommend the translations of Lawrence C. Braceland SJ and Mary Eugenia Laker SSND: *Aelred of Rievaulx: Spiritual Friendship*, ed. Marsha L. Dutton, trans. Lawrence Braceland (Collegeville MN: Liturgical Press, 2010) and *Spiritual Friendship: Aelred of Rievaulx*, trans. by M. Eugenia Laker with commentary by Dennis Billy CSsR (Notre Dame IN: Ave Maria Press, 2008). The latter includes helpful summaries and commentaries of sections within the text. To read the original text in Latin, visit: https://www.documentacatholicaomnia.eu/02m/1110-1167,_Aelredus_Rievallensis_Abbas,_De_Spirituali_Amicitia_Liber,_MLT.pdf

6. *Martyrology of Oengus the Culdee*, translated by Whitley Stokes, D.C.L. (London: Harrison & Sons, 1905), 65.

7. John O'Donohue, *Anam Cara: Spiritual Wisdom from the Celtic World* (New York: Bantam Books, 1997), 35. My emphasis added.

8. Anamchara Fellowship is a Religious Community in the Episcopal Church with a Celtic Christian spirit and has canonical recognition by the House of Bishops Committee on the Religious Life. Books on Celtic Spirituality and Soul Friends include Esther De Waal, *The Celtic Way of Prayer: The Recovery of the Religious Imagination* (New York: Image, 1999), Oliver Davies, *Celtic Spirituality* (Mahwah NJ: Paulist Press, 2000), Edward C. Sellner, *The Celtic Soul Friend: A Trusted Guide for Today* (Notre Dame IN: Ave Maria Press, 2002), Edward C. Sellner, *Stories of the Celtic Soul Friends: Their Meaning for Today* (Mahwah NJ: Paulist Press, 2004), and Mary C. Earle, *Celtic Christian Spirituality: Essential Writings Annotated & Explained* (Nashville TN: SkyLight Paths, 2011).

9. John O'Donohue, *Anam Cara: Spiritual Wisdom from the Celtic World* (New York: Bantam Books, 1997), 36.

10. John Cassian, *Conferences,* 16.3, https://www.newadvent.org/fathers/350816.htm.

11. *Martyrology of Oengus the Culdee*, 65.

12. Apparently, Alfred combed and trimmed the saint's hair and beard and cut his fingernails. According to tradition, Alfred would place the hairs of the saint on coals within a thurible, where they would shine like gold rather than shrivel and burn. Like the bodies of many saints, Cuthbert's body did not decompose. Located in Durham Cathedral, Cuthbert's body remained incorrupt for over eight centuries, exhibiting miraculous powers akin to the Tibetan Buddhist phenomenon of the Rainbow Body. See *Symeon of Durham*, edited by T. Arnold, as cited by Aelred Squire, *Aelred of Rievaulx: A Study* (London: SPCK, 1969), 5. For more on the Rainbow Body, see Francis V. Tiso, *Rainbow Body and Resurrection: Spiritual Attainment, the Dissolution of the Material Body, and the Case of Khenpo A Chö* (Berkeley: North Atlantic Books, 2016).

13. Anselm Hoste, "A Survey of the Unedited Work of Laurence of Durham and an Edition of his Letter to Aelred of Rievaulx," *Sacris Erudiri* 11 (1960): 263.

14. A paraphrase of the proverb, "A young prince must prepare for war good companions and give rings" from Maxims II, a gnomic poem contained in a copy of the *Anglo-Saxon Chronicle* in MS Cotton Tiberius B.i. *Anglo-Saxon Spirituality*, translated by Robert Boenig (Mahwah NJ: Paulist Press, 2000), 264. The ring served as a symbol of loyalty in Anglo-Saxon culture.

15. Martin Thornton, *English Spirituality: An Outline of Ascetical Theology According to the English Pastoral Tradition* (London: SPCK, 1963), 49.

16. Thornton sees this characteristic particularly in English medieval mystics Margery Kempe and Richard Rolle "and possibly Aelred of Rievaulx as well." Martin Thornton, *English Spirituality: An Outline of Ascetical Theology According to the English Pastoral Tradition* (London: SPCK, 1963), 49.

17. Maxims II, *Anglo-Saxon Spirituality*, 264.

18. During his lifetime, Aelred was known mostly as an historian who authored *The Life of St. Edward the King and Confessor,* one of the last Anglo-Saxon English kings. "Living in a multi-ethnic Anglo-Saxon and Franco-Norman family," Pierre-André Burton writes, "must have made Aelred particularly sensitive to both the singular challenge and the immense richness represented by the harmonious cohabitation of individuals of different temperaments and multiple cultural origins." Pierre-André Burton OCSO, *Aelred of Rievaulx 1110–1167: An Existential and Spiritual Biography,* trans. Christopher Coski (Collegeville MN: Liturgical Press, 2020), 97.

19. Aelred of Rievaulx, *Mirror of Charity* 3.40; *Mirror of Charity*, trans. Elizabeth Connor OCSO (Kalamazoo MI: Cistercian Publications, 1990), 301.

20. Marcus Tullis Cicero, *De Officiis*, 1.56.

21. An adaptation of the following quote from Cicero's Letter to Varro: "If you have a garden in your library, you have it all." Cicero, *Epistulae ad Familiares* 9.4.1.

22. Cicero, *De Amicitia* 6.20-21.

23. Giovanni Zuanazzi, "Introduction," in Aelredo di Rievaulx, *L'amicizia spirtuale,* trans. Giovanni Zuanazzi (Rome: Città Nouva, 1997), 11, as cited in Pierre-André Burton, *Aelred of Rievaulx 1110-1167,* 101.

24. Cicero, *De Amicitia,* 18.65.

25. Cicero, *De Amicitia,* 22.83.

26. Joseph A. Stewart-Sicking reflects on Aelred's four qualities (loyalty, patience, good intention, and discretion) within the context of Alexander John Shaia's four-path journey of change, suffering, joy, and service. In my distillation of Book III, I explicitly correlate the four qualities with the four paths. See Joseph A. Stewart-Sicking, *Spiritual Friendship after Religion: Walking with People while the Rules Are Changing* (New York: Morehouse Publishing, 2016); Alexander John Shaia with Michelle L. Gaugy, *Heart and Mind: The Four-Gospel Journey for Radical Transformation* (Preston Australia: Mosaic Press, 2013).

27. Cicero, *De Amicitia,* 26.97.

28. Cicero, *De Officiis,* 1.56.

29. Bishop Curry, "Holding on to Hope: A National Service for Healing and Wholeness," Nov 1, 2020. https://www.episcopalnewsservice.org/pressre leases/presiding-bishop-michael-currys-sermon-from-holding-on-to-hope-a-national-service-for-healing-and-wholeness/

30. Bernard of Clairvaux, *On Loving God* 3.7; *Bernard of Clairvaux: Selected Works,* trans. G. R. Evans (Mahwah NJ: Paulist Press, 1987), 179.

31. The Rule of St. Benedict, 40.

32. Also, the presence of a class of monks called oblates contributed to the growing laxity, especially since many, though not all, oblates were essentially given to the monastery because their parents could not afford to raise them.

33. Reform movements included the Cluniac Reform based in Cluny, France (909) and the Cistercian Reform based in Citeaux (1098).

34. See E. Ann Matter, *The Voice of My Beloved: The Song of Songs in Western Medieval Christianity* (Philadelphia: University of Philadelphia Press, 1990).

35. Bernard of Clairvaux, *Song of Songs* Sermon 4, in *Bernard of Clairvaux: Selected* Works, translated by G. R. Evans (Mahwah NJ: Paulist Press, 1987), 224–226. For more on Bernard's and Aelred's reading of the Song of Songs, see *A Companion to the Song of Songs in the History of Spirituality,* edited by Timothy Robinson (Leiden: Brill, 2021), especially chapter 4 (Catherine Rose Cavadini, "The Cistercian Song", 101-122) and chapter 6 (Ann W. Astell, "The Song of Songs in Aelred of Rievaulx's Liturgical Preaching," 157 - 188).

36. Columban Heaney OSCO, *The Cistercian Spirit: A Symposium in Memory of Thomas Merton,* edited by M. Basil Pennington OCSO (Spencer MA: Cistercian Publications, 1970), 166–167.

37. According to the Hebrew Scriptures, the Sabbath is to be observed not only on the seventh day of each week, but also on the last year of a seven-year span and the last year of a fifty-year span (after seven-times-seven years). Leviticus 25.

38. Aelred, *Mirror of Charity* 3:1-5.

39. Aelred, *Spiritual Friendship* 1.35; *Spiritual Friendship: The Classic Text with a Spiritual Commentary by Dennis Billy, C.S.s.R.,* translated by Mary Eugenia Laker (Notre Dame IN: Ave Maria Press, 2008), 39. Also, Aelred says, "Let love of self, then, be man's first sabbath." *Mirror of Charity* 3.2.

40. C. S. Lewis, *Letter (19 April 1951)* in *Letters of C. S. Lewis,* ed. W. H. Lewis and Walter Hooper (New York: HarperOne, 2017), 230.

41. Bernard of Clairvaux, *On Loving God* 3.7.

42. Thomas Merton, *New Seeds of Contemplation* (New York: New Directions, 1972), 75. Merton was a Trappist monk, which means he was part of the Order of Cistercians of the Strict Observance (OCSO).

43. Some scholars argue that Bernard's references to stones and trees should be understood metaphorically, not literally. See Emero Stiegman, "'Woods and Stones' & 'The Shade of Trees' in the Mysticism of Saint Bernard" in *Truth as Gift: Studies in Honor of John R. Sommerfeldt,* ed. Marsha Dutton et. al. (Kalamazoo MI: Cistercian Publications, 2004), 321–354.

44. Aelred of Rievaulx, *Jesus at the Age of Twelve* 17 (p. 22); *Aelred of Rievaulx: Treatises & Pastoral Prayer,* trans. Theodore Berkeley OCSO (Kalamazoo MI: Cistercian Publications, 1971), 22. The first time I visited the abbey ruins of Rievaulx was a couple days after completing my training as a certified Forest Therapy Guide through the Association of Nature and Forest Therapy at the Broughton Sanctuary in Yorkshire. I do not deny that this experience has colored my reading of Aelred.

45. While the references to the natural world and especially trees within Bernard's letter and Aelred's treatise may be appropriately understood as symbolic, they nonetheless invite readers to reflect on the possibility of friendship with nature. See "Spiritual Practice III–Befriending a Tree" in the Appendix.

46. An acute distillation of Aelred's *Pastoral Prayer* in *Aelred of Rievaulx: Treatises & Pastoral Prayer,* 103–118.

BERNARD'S LETTER TO AELRED, DISTILLED

Dear Brother Aelred,

The greatest virtue of the saints is humility; and you have indeed demonstrated humility by offering a plethora of excuses to refrain from the spiritual writing project that I asked you to pursue. You say that you are an unlearned and illiterate man who arrived in the monastery via the kitchen rather than the classroom. You say that you are a country bumpkin living among rocks and hills, working for your daily bread by the sweat of your brow with axe and mallet;[1] and you insist that such circumstances have taught you more about silence than about speaking or writing eloquently.

I hear and understand all these excuses; however, they only fan the flame of my desire for you to complete the spiritual writing that I asked you to pursue. Whatever knowledge you did not gain from the classroom you have clearly gained from the school of the Holy Spirit and that knowledge will prove to be the most nutritious knowledge of all. And I remind you that true humility is also expressed in obedience.

So now, I am not only *asking* you to write; I am *ordering and commanding* you to write because I know your words will bring spiritual nourishment. Just as you previously provided food as a steward in the royal house of the king of Scotland, so too will your words now feed those who are hungry with the Word of God in the house of our divine king.

I appreciated your description of the ruggedness of the mountains and the depths of the valleys and the cragginess of the rocks where you live. My friend, you have discovered things in the woods that you would have never found in books. Stones and trees have taught you things that you would have never learned from your schoolteachers. Your experience of simply sitting under the shade of trees during a hot summer day after hours of manual labor has given you wisdom that ought to be shared. So, don't blush out of fear of being presumptuous or out of fear of arousing envy in others. No one ever published anything useful without causing some envy; and certainly no one can consider you presumptuous for simply obeying your abbot.

And so, I order you in the Name of Jesus Christ and in the Spirit of God to stop putting off this project. I suggest that you include this letter at the beginning of your book so that if anyone is displeased with the book they can blame me, not you.

Your beloved friend in Christ and your abbot,

Fr. Bernard of Clairvaux

---

1. The axe and mallet were the tools that Aelred used in building up the church and monastery at Rievaulx. Manual labor is a key component of Cistercian spirituality.

PROLOGUE

Humility is indeed the virtue of the saints,
but I hesitate to call my obedience in writing "humility"
because whatever humility I can claim for myself
is derived from my lack of virtue and expertise.[1]
Not only am I inexperienced in writing,
but I am also a poor speaker,
often tripping over my words.

When I moved from the kitchen to the monastery,
I changed my location not my locution.[2]
But you're not interested in my excuses,
and you have entrusted me
with your confidence and affection.

So, whatever wisdom I've gained from
the mountains and valleys,
the stones and trees,
and even from the honey and oil with which I cooked,
I have tried to write in this reflection

on belovedness and friendship.

If any good comes out of this reflection,
it is only because of the grace
of the divine Lover and your prayers for me.

Before I learned the meaning of true friendship,
I was often deceived by its artifice,
tossed to and fro by the waves of passion and lust.[3]
When I read Cicero's treatise,
I became fascinated by what seemed to be
a sophisticated formula for friendship.
After entering the monastery at Rievaulx
and immersing myself in a life of prayer,
Cicero's book began to lose its luster
as did most things that were not
dipped in the sweet honey of Christ's love.

In the following three books,
I have attempted to dip Cicero's wisdom on friendship
in that same sweet honey.
The first book is about the nature and origin of friendship;
the second is about its excellence;
and the third is about how it can
best be practiced and preserved.

If any of this is helpful, thank God, not me.
If any of this seems to be superfluous, please forgive me.
I could only devote so much time to this project
amidst my other responsibilities at Rievaulx.

---

1. This prologue synthesizes and distills Aelred's prologue to *Mirror of Charity* and *Spiritual Friendship*.

2. Although Aelred's scholastic education in Durham may have been cut short, he would have been better educated than most. As steward of the royal household in Scotland, he oversaw work in the kitchen, but also would have received top-grade tutoring alongside Prince Henry. So, his claim of being "unlearned and illiterate" is an expression of extreme and even false modesty. Such claims to modesty were a common medieval trope.

3. Some historians have suggested that Aelred was a homosexual, thus granting him the title "the gay abbot of Rievaulx" and the patron saint of the currently defunct LGBTQ+ advocacy group of the Episcopal Church called "Integrity." Although modern claims about Aelred's homosexuality remain conjecture, they have, according to his definitive biographer Pierre-André Burton, "breathed new life into Aelredian studies." Burton, *Aelred of Rievaulx 1110-1167*, 27. I like to imagine that Aelred would have found a degree of pride in learning that he would become a patron and protector of a community persistently marginalized by the church. At the 1987 national convention of Integrity, the group passed a resolution "to regularly observe his feast [Jan 12], promote his veneration and seek before the heavenly throne of grace the support of his prayers on behalf of justice and acceptance for lesbians and gay men." See John Boswell, *Christianity, Social Tolerance, and Homosexuality: Gay People in Western Europe from the Beginning of the Christian Era to the Fourteenth Century* (Chicago: Chicago University Press, 1980), Brian Patrick McGuire, *Brother and Lover: Aelred of Rievaulx* (New York: Crossroad Press, 1994). For a rebuttal of Boswell's and McGuire's theory, see Marsha L. Dutton, "Aelred of Rievaulx on Friendship, Chastity, and Sex: The Sources," *Cistercian Studies Quarterly* 29 (1994): 121–196, Marsha L. Dutton, "The Invented Sexual History of Aelred of Rievaulx: A Review Article," *American Benedictine Review* 47 (1996): 414–432.

BOOK 1

AELRED

Here we are. You and me.
And I hope Christ makes three.
Now that we are free from the chatter of the crowd,
let us relish this opportunity.
A little while ago, I sensed that you wanted
to speak with me more intently about something,
but you were drowned out
by the clamor of the louder monks.
Now that we are alone, tell me,
what's on your heart and mind?

IVO

Thank you, Father, for your attentiveness.
Clearly, the spirit of love has revealed to you
what I have been seeking for quite some time now:
to meet with you alone and learn from you
about the gift of spiritual friendship.

You see, I have read Cicero's treatise
On Friendship and admire its wisdom,
but ever since I experienced the love of God in Christ,
I have found that most things are stale
if they are not dipped in the sweet honey of that love.[1]

AELRED
I certainly understand.
However, instead of me teaching you,
let's discuss this subject together
so we can learn from each other.
Let's pour out our shared wisdom
and drink it in together.
Where shall we begin?

IVO
Perhaps we could begin
with a basic definition of friendship,
which can serve as a kind of canvas
for our conversation.

AELRED
Very well, let's consider Cicero's definition,
at least as a starting point.
Friendship, according to Cicero, is
a *special harmony of shared interests
coupled with goodwill and affection.*

IVO
This is a helpful definition,
but honestly, it seems too broad to me.
How can we understand this definition
in the light of Christ?

AELRED
Although this definition may not be entirely sufficient,
let's start by unpacking it a bit.

Friends are companions who enjoy
a common accord in relation to shared interests,
not necessarily agreeing on everything,
but generally singing in the same key, so to speak.

This harmony is coupled with affection,
which is the enjoyment of simply being
in each other's presence,
and goodwill, which involves wishing
for the other person's ultimate good.[2]

When we wish for what is good for our friends,
we become guardians of their souls,
rejoicing with them in their joys
and weeping in their sorrows.
As best we can, we try to feel
our friends' feelings as if they were our own.
Friendship, therefore, is a virtue
by which spirits become fastened together
by a love that makes one out of many.
This oneness in love is eternal.
In fact, of all human relationships,
friendship alone continues to persist
practically unchanged in Heaven.[3]
The wise King Solomon affirmed this
when he said, "A friend loves *forever*."[4]

IVO
This kind of empathetic goodwill that you describe,

this feeling of our friend's feelings
as if they were our own,
sounds challenging to practice and attain.

AELRED
Perhaps, but aren't most great things
challenging to attain?
We ought to seek all the great virtues,
knowing that we will be blessed
in the process of seeking them.
Jesus said, "Ask and you shall receive.
Seek and you shall find."[5]

So, let's not be afraid to ask for
and to seek the virtue of true friendship
from the Giver of all good things.
God, who gives generously to those who ask,
has caused the light of true friendship
to shine upon Christians and non-Christians alike.
Consider Pylades and Orestes who did not know Christ,
but who both experienced the love of true friendship
when Pylades offered his life to save Orestes
as he was facing capital punishment.[6]

And recall the example of the Christian soldier Didymus
who demonstrated this same love
when he rescued the virgin Theodora
from prostitution and subsequently
suffered a beheading.[7]

We see this light of true friendship shine brightest
whenever someone shows love

by seeking the good of a friend
even to the point of putting
their own safety and wellbeing at risk.
"There is no greater love," Jesus said,
"than to lay down one's life for a friend."[8]

IVO
So, are love and friendship essentially the same thing?

AELRED
No. Not at all.
There is certainly a difference.
We are to receive more people into the bosom of love
than into the embrace of friendship.
Remember, Christ called us to love
not only our friends, but also our enemies.
We strive to love our enemies,
but we don't entrust our hearts and personal secrets
to them the way we do with our close friends,
who also share those same intimacies with us.

IVO
What about friendships among sinful,
selfish, and greedy people?
Can sinful and greedy people
experience the joy of friendship too?

AELRED
I honestly hesitate to call such relationships "friendships,"
since true friendship is always rooted in virtue, not vice.[9]
One cannot authentically wish for someone else's good
if they are not already seeking

ST. AELRED OF RIEVAULX

that which is good and virtuous for themselves.[10]
However, since sinful and greedy people may experience
some similar feelings of harmony between themselves,
let's make a distinction between
different kinds of friendships.

There are spiritual friendships,
but there are also *carnal* friendships
and *worldly* friendships.
Carnal friendships thrive on an unhealthy
harmony of violence and vice, not virtue,
while worldly friendships are
concerned only with personal gain.
Once you remove the possibility
of selfish gain from a worldly friendship,
the relationship immediately falls apart.

Such "fair-weather friends" disappear
as soon as difficulties arise,
and whenever the so-called benefits
of the relationship are threatened, they leave.[11]
The benefit and reward of true friendship
is the friendship itself.

When Jesus called his followers to bear fruit,
he was referring to the fruit of friendship and love,
which is fruit that persists unto eternity.[12]
The reward of friendship is simply the privilege
to participate in that joyful harmony of shared interests
coupled with affection and goodwill.
Now that we have returned to the definition
from which we began,
do you feel enough has been said

about the nature of friendship itself?

IVO
Yes, your explanation about the nature of friendship
has been helpful. Thank you.
But before we must go to dinner,
I'd like to learn from you about the origin of friendship.
Did friendship originate naturally or accidentally
or was it imposed by some outside law?

AELRED
Friendship emerged naturally in the sense that
our desire for friendship is part of our human nature,
and our experience of friendship
makes us long for it even more.

We have been made in the image of God,
who is a unity of three persons.
So, it is natural for us to seek unity in diversity,
to bring multiple parts together as one.
Just look at the natural world.
Look at the river.
Do you see only one stone under the water?
Look at the forest.
Is there only one tree?

IVO
No, the river contains a vast array of stones
and the forest, a glorious assortment of trees.

AELRED
Yes, because the stones enjoy
the camaraderie of fellow stones,

and trees the company of fellow trees.
And watch how animals play with each other
and so often delight in each other's presence,
loving nothing more than the experience of friendship.
And who can embody friendship more wonderfully
than that beloved animal whom we call "man's best *friend*"?[13]

Friendship also thrives among the Angels.
Although God has ordered the Angels
according to echelon,
they do not fall prey to envy because
the gift of friendship and affection
always overrides competition.

When God finished making the universe,
he realized there was something missing.
Even in God's Paradise,
before sin had entered the world,
God saw that something was *not* good.
He saw that man was alone and without a friend.
So, with perfect flourish,
God added his finishing touch:
human friendship,
the cherry on top of all creation.

Beautifully and brilliantly,
God made the first human friend,
appropriately from the side of the first human
—not the head nor the feet—
to clearly teach us that in friendship
there is no superior or inferior,
that there is no room for envy in the equality of friendship.

Tragically, when sin entered the world,
envy crept into our relationships,
accompanied by the toxic fear of scarcity.
Now when we wish good things for our friends,
we can so easily become threatened by a zero-sum game,
afraid that good things for our friends
might mean fewer good things for ourselves.

However, true friendship persists
as wholly good and natural,
as the perfect icing on the cake of all creation.
Like wisdom and virtue,
we ought to seek friendship wholeheartedly,
knowing that it can never be entirely abused.

IVO
Are you really saying that wisdom, friendship,
and virtue can never be entirely abused?
If so, I'm confused,
because don't people often abuse wisdom
whenever they use it to puff up their egos
or to greedily steal money
or to put others down?

AELRED
That's not real wisdom, Ivo.
Even if someone seems to utilize wisdom for selfish gain,
they are, in fact, foolish and not wise at all.
Similarly, if someone boasts about
attaining a particular virtue, like chastity,
such boasting reveals that the supposed virtue is,
in reality, a vice.

IVO
Ok, but please forgive me for not understanding
your comparison between wisdom and friendship.
The conflation of the two doesn't make sense to me.

AELRED
On one level, they are different
and yet, if you consider carefully
what we have said about friendship,
you will find that friendship and wisdom
are not only similar;
they are essentially the same.

IVO
Wow. I will admit that
I am amazed by your conclusion,
and yet also not convinced.

AELRED
Remember the wisdom of King Solomon,
who said, "A friend loves forever."
In friendship, eternity blossoms,
truth radiates, and love thrives.
Do you really want to separate the name of wisdom
from eternity, truth, and love?

IVO
Then are you suggesting that we conflate all these things?
Should we say of friendship what John,
the friend of Jesus, said of love,
that "God is friendship"?[14]

AELRED
Oh, I like that!

IVO
I like it too, but didn't you just say
love and friendship are not the same thing?

AELRED
Yes, I did and, at the same time,
I'm not afraid to say that whatever is true of love
is also true of friendship,
so "those who abide in friendship,
abide in God, and God in them."[15]

As I said just moments ago,
we are to receive more people
into the bosom of love
than into the embrace of friendship
for friendship is a particular kind of love.

This will become more and more clear when
we discuss the fruits and the practice of friendship.
Now if we have said enough about
the nature and origin of friendship,
let's schedule a time later
to discuss the other questions you had.

IVO
Because I'm so eager to continue our conversation,
I must admit that I'm very annoyed
we need to stop right now,
but I understand that it's time for dinner
and our presence at the refectory is mandatory.

I also know that there are other brothers
who have a right to your care and attention.

---

1. Here Aelred attributes to Ivo what he himself expresses in the Prologue: the desire to dip Cicero's wisdom in the sweet honey of Christ's love.
2. C. S. Lewis describes biblical love for neighbor as wishing for their good, explaining, "Love is not affectionate feeling, but a steady wishing for the loved person's ultimate good as far as it can be obtained." C. S. Lewis, *God in the Dock: Essays on Theology and Ethics* (Grand Rapids MI: William B. Eerdmans, 1972), 49. This description of love as wishing for someone else's good is also found in Aristotle's *Nicomachean Ethics* 1156b, which Aelred likely did not read.
3. St. Anselm of Canterbury (1093–1109) said that the only pleasure on earth which survives, essentially unaltered, in heaven is the pleasure of friendship. R.W. Southern, *St. Anselm: A Portrait in a Landscape* (Cambridge: Cambridge University Press, 1992), 155, 161.
4. Proverbs 17:17.
5. Matthew 7:7.
6. According to the *Oresteia* trilogy by Aeschylus, Orestes was facing capital punishment after killing his adulterous mother Clytemnestra. However, Pylades offered his life to protect his friend by saying, "I am Orestes," thus demonstrating the highest form of self-giving love.
7. Ambrose, *On Virgins* 2.4.22-32.
8. John 15:13.
9. C. S. Lewis recalls the wisdom of "the ancients" when he describes friendship as "a school of virtue." However, he also warns that friendship can likewise become a school of vice, making good people better and bad people worse. Lewis, *The Four Loves* (New York: Harcourt Brace Jovanovich, 1960), 115.
10. In *Mirror of Charity*, Aelred explains, "When the Scriptures say, 'You shall love your neighbor as yourself, it is clear that you ought also to love yourself. This...should be inherent to our nature." Aelred, *Mirror of Charity*, 3.2.
11. In Book 8 of his *Nicomachean Ethics*, Aristotle also delineates friendship into the following three categories: friendships of pleasure (akin to Aelred's "carnal friendships"), friendships of utility (Aelred's "worldly friendships"), and friendships of virtue ("spiritual friendship"). According to Dutton, Aelred did not know Aristotle's *Ethics*, but was likely familiar with his ideas through the writings of Cicero. Marsha L. Dutton, *Aelred of Rievaulx: Spiritual Friendship* (Collegeville MN: Liturgical Press, 2010), 31.
12. John 15:16.
13. Aelred was familiar with St. Brigid, whose friendship with a dog, according to legend, led to a miraculous multiplication of food for the

hungry poor. "The Irish Life of Brigit," in Oliver Davies, *Celtic Spirituality* (Mahwah NJ: Paulist Press, 1999), 141-142.

14. "God is Love." 1 John 4:16. St. Anselm also believed that friendship penetrates the nature of God in its sharing in the mutual love of the three persons of the Trinity. R. W. Southern, *St. Anselm*, 155.

15. "Those who abide in love abide in God and God abides in them." 1 John 4:16.

BOOK II

AELRED
What's bothering you, Walter?
You seem clearly distressed.

WALTER
Yes, I *am* distressed.
These annoying people keep occupying your time
while we, who deserve your primary attention,
can't get a word in edgewise.

AELRED
I understand, but we must
show kindness to everyone,
including people whom
we experience as annoying;
but now that they're gone,
we can appreciate our shared solitude even more,
since solitude is enriched
when it is preceded by company.

You've heard it said that hunger
is the best sauce for any dish;
and no spice can improve wine
in the same way that a strong thirst
can enhance one's enjoyment
of a simple glass of water.
Similarly, our soulful conversation
can now be more thoroughly enjoyed
after an intense longing for it.
Tell me, what's on your heart?

WALTER
I'm wondering if you remember the conversation
you had with Ivo about spiritual friendship.

AELRED
Of course, I remember that conversation fondly,
almost as fondly as I remember Ivo himself.
Although my beloved Ivo has passed on from this life,
he remains very close to me in spirit,
almost as if he never died at all.
Spiritual friends remain present when they are absent,
rich when poor, strong when weak,
and alive even after they have died.
I can still see his smiling eyes and hear his happy words.
I'm glad my conversation with him was recorded; however, I
seem to have misplaced the parchment
upon which our conversation was written.

WALTER
Yes, I know.
That is partly why I've been so eager to speak with you.
The parchment has been discovered

and I'd love for us to review it together
to see if any points need to be polished,
reexamined, or expanded.

AELRED

Sure. I would be happy to do that with you.

WALTER

You and Ivo discussed the nature of friendship
in such a satisfying way.
Now I'm wondering if we can explore
what fruits and gifts remain in store
for those who cultivate the practice of friendship.

AELRED

There is nothing more sacred or sweet
than the gift of friendship itself,
which bears fruit both in this life and the next,
manifesting all the virtues
while also protecting us from all vices.

We cannot experience true happiness
unless we have someone with whom
we can share our insights, confess our secrets,
and celebrate our achievements.

A friend is like another self,
like a mirror reflecting our true joy and freedom.
Imagine a drug that makes your highs even higher
while simultaneously easing the burdens of your lows.
Now imagine that this miracle drug
is also healthy and good for you!
This is friendship,

which the wise teacher calls "the medicine of life."[1]

It is through this medicine that we learn
how to enjoy the most profound friendship of all:
our friendship with the One who says to us,
"I no longer call you servants.
I now call you my friends."[2]

WALTER
Wow! It's almost like you are saying
that we are not yet fully alive
without the experience of friendship.

I'd love to hear more about how
this medicine of spiritual friendship
can help us enjoy the most profound friendship of all.

But look, here comes our earnest friend Gratian,
who might benefit from this conversation as well.
He seems to be nearly obsessed
with the subject of friendship.

GRATIAN
Please forgive me for imposing,
but if you are discussing friendship,
then I would indeed benefit from this conversation.

If you weren't exaggerating when you just said
that I was obsessed with the subject of friendship, Walter,
then I'm wondering why you didn't include me
in this conversation from the beginning!

Father Aelred, even though I may have missed

part of the spiritual feast you have been serving,
please continue to set your dishes on the table
so that I may receive at least some nourishment.

AELRED
Don't worry, Gratian.
The most important matters have not yet been discussed.
We were just about to discuss the way spiritual friendship
helps us to enjoy the most profound friendship of all.
Spiritual friendship includes
truth, joy, goodwill, and affection;
and Christ is the source and perfection of all these.

When we experience spiritual friendship,
we deepen our experience of Christ.
Experiencing spiritual friendship
is like having a kiss blown in our direction,
directly from Christ's lips.

GRATIAN
Friendship as a Christ-blown kiss?
Beautiful! Please say more about this!

AELRED
Well, I can probably explain this best
by describing the three different kinds of kisses:
There is the physical kiss,
the spiritual kiss,
and the mystical kiss.

The physical kiss is the gentle pressing together
of lips between lovers or perhaps close friends.
In a kiss, two breaths meet and mingle

and become one.[3]

Let's be careful not to misuse or abuse
this expression of intimate love
in any perverse or inappropriate ways,
like Judas who twisted this symbol of love
into a hateful sign of betrayal.

The spiritual kiss is not made
by any physical contact of the mouth
but by the affections of the heart.
Do you ever feel like you just exchanged
a warm and loving kiss with someone
with whom you had no direct physical contact at all,
as if the spiritual harmony between you two
was almost palpable?

That is Christ pursing his lips and blowing you a kiss!

GRATIAN
Lovely! And what's the mystical kiss?

AELRED
That's the experience of mystical union with Christ,
which the poet of the Song of Song longs for when he prays,
"Let him kiss me with the kisses of his mouth."[4]

The mystical kiss is not just a kiss
blown in our direction.
It is the soul-seizing kiss of Christ
which the poet describes when he says,
"His left hand is under my head
and his right arm embraces me."[5]

The spiritual kiss of friendship prepares us
for this mind-blowing, heart-bursting
and soul-seizing kiss of the divine.[6]

GRATIAN
Friendship as a preparation for the mystical kiss?
I honestly thought of friendship as little more
than a happy relationship
between two people with similar interests.

WALTER
If you were as familiar as I am
with Father Aelred's previous conversation with Ivo
you would have known that friendship is
"a special harmony of shared interests
coupled with goodwill and affection."

You would have known that goodwill is expressed
when friends seek each other's ultimate good;
and some say that we ought to seek our friend's good
even if that involves sacrificing
money, honor, and reputation.

And now, since I know Gratian often lives up to his name
by showing excessive *graciousness* to his friends,
I ask this question on his behalf:
What are the limits of sacrifice in friendship?
I ask because I'm worried that if Gratian keeps making
such extreme sacrifices for his friends,
he will end up destitute and dis*graced*.

GRATIAN
I appreciate your thoughtful concern for me, Walter,

and the only reason I'm not going to clap back
and make fun of your own silly-sounding name
is because I'm interested in Father Aelred's response.

AELRED
The limits of sacrifice in friendship?
Christ himself said,
"There is no greater love
than to lay down one's life for a friend."
Being willing to die for each other
is the limit of sacrifice in friendship.

GRATIAN
Sacrificing one's life
is the greatest possible expression of friendship.
So, despite Walter's teasing,
I apparently still have not yet reached
the zenith of gracious sacrifice in my friendships.

WALTER
I'm wondering if such sacrificial friendship
is possible among the sinful and wicked.

AELRED
Perhaps, but I would not call sacrificial behavior
among the sinful an expression of friendship,
because true friendship cannot exist among the wicked.

GRATIAN
Then who can friendship exist among?

AELRED
Friendship cannot truly exist *except* among the good.

GRATIAN

Well then, why are we even talking about
friendship at all since I don't think we are
particularly good? In fact, I think Walter and I
might even be a bit wicked.

AELRED

Let me unpack what I mean by "good."
A good person is not a perfect person,
but rather someone who is seeking
to live a good and godly life.
Such a person would not ask someone else
to do wrong nor would they respond affirmatively
to someone else's request for them to do wrong.
Among such good people, friendship can be perfected.
In fact, for them, friendship serves
as a powerful support and encouragement
on the transformative path towards good and godly living.

But those who do wrong to please their friends
are foolishly falling towards destruction.
They guard someone else's honor while betraying
their own.
They fall prey to the grifters
who use the guise of "friendship"
to manipulate others and get what they want.

WALTER

Yes, I've experienced such manipulative behavior
and consequently suffered anxiety, betrayal, and grief.
I've almost been tempted to agree with the Stoics
who say that friendship should be avoided entirely
since it can be the cause of so much pain.[7]

GRATIAN

Walter, if avoiding friendship altogether
were a serious option for us,
then why would we be having this conversation?
Our desire for friendship seems healthy and good
and frankly undeniable.

AELRED

Indeed. For those of us who are made
in the image of the Triune God
in whom holy friendship ceaselessly flows,
a natural desire for spiritual friendship
will remain undeniable.

Avoiding this part of ourselves would be like
avoiding the very image of God
in which we are made.
Let the Stoics do what they want,
but let's not be so foolish ourselves.

Those who take friendship out of life
are like those who try to take the sun
and all the stars out of the sky.
Cicero said that the gods have given us
nothing more pleasant than friendship.

I'm so sorry, Walter,
that you have been hurt by others
who have used friendship as a weapon
and tool for manipulation;
and I hope our friendship can bring
some healing and restoration.
Although friendship might be

the cause of some anxiety and even grief,
that is not a sufficient reason to avoid it entirely.

All of life includes some anxiety and grief,
but that doesn't mean we ought to stop living.
The Stoics would have likely considered
Christ and St. Paul fools
since their friendships with others
clearly caused anxiety and grief
within their hearts.

King David's spy Hushai
must have experienced severe anxiety
when he served as an undercover informant
among Absalom's advisors
for the sake of his dear friend and king.[8]

As I shared with Ivo,
even the stones and trees
appreciate company.
So also do the beasts of the field.
Even more than stones and trees and beasts,
we who are made in God's image
seek and desire friendship
because it is through such friendships
that God's image shines most brightly.

And we brutally corrupt
the image of God in which we are made
whenever we use our friends for selfish gain
or when we manipulate others
under the guise of friendship.

WALTER
There are clearly some kinds of friendship
we ought to avoid and others we ought to seek.
Will you please tell us exactly which ones to avoid
and which ones to seek and cherish?

AELRED
Sure. I will try to answer in just a few words.
We want to avoid friendships of advantage,
which we have already discussed,
and which really do not deserve
the name "friendship" at all
since they are simply selfish people
trying to objectify each other.

There are many glorious advantages
that naturally flow from friendship,
but we do not seek friendship for this purpose.
We seek friendship for the gift of the friendship itself.
We want to avoid what I call
infantile and possessive friendships.

These are the friendships characterized
by unrestrained affection and passion,
which cause us to seek control
and possession of another person.

Although affection is an important part of friendship,
it needs to be coupled with goodwill;
and when we authentically seek someone else's good,
we become willing to let go
and let others be themselves,
without controlling or insisting

we know what's best for them.

Look at the mist rising from the river valley!
It's so beautiful and so attractive
that we might want to try to capture it in a bottle,
but so much of its beauty lies in its ephemerality
and in our inability to control or contain it.

Likewise with our friends,
let us learn to love them with affection
but also with enough goodwill
to let them be themselves
and perhaps, at times, to let them go.

Sometimes this might mean that we ourselves
need to give them space
and temporarily fly away like the mist.
Sometimes this might even mean
that we lay down our very lives
in order for their souls to truly thrive.

GRATIAN
Wow! You lost me with that last part.
That sounds extreme.
Can you say more about that for us?

AELRED
Remember what I said earlier
about the limits of sacrifice in friendships?
"There is no greater love
than to lay down one's life for a friend."

WALTER
Yes, but you also said that it is foolish
for people to do wrong and thus dishonor themselves
for the purpose of honoring a friend.

AELRED
When it comes to laying down one's life for a friend,
we are talking about the precious life of the body.
When it comes to doing wrong for a friend,
we are talking about the soul;
and we must not destroy the soul
for the sake of a friend.

GRATIAN
Thank you, Walter, for asking that question
because I was starting to get confused,
and Father's response is helping me to understand.

But I'm still wondering:
how do we know if our sacrifices
are threatening our bodies or our souls?
And how do we discern when it's appropriate
to make such extreme sacrifices?

AELRED
These are important questions
that remain to be discussed.
However, as you can see,
our brothers have arrived to hustle me off
to other business...

WALTER

For the record, I leave this conversation begrudgingly,
but I hope the time between this conversation
and our next one won't be as long
as the time between Father's conversation
with Ivo and today.
Let's plan to meet here tomorrow and,
Gratian my friend, try not to be late next time.

---

1. Ben Sirach 6:16.
2. John 15:15.
3. The traditional Aotearoa New Zealand greeting among friends in Māori involves the pressing together of noses and foreheads. This greeting is called Hongi, which is Māori for "sharing of breath."
4. Song of Songs 1:1.
5. Song of Songs 2:6.
6. Aelred's three categories of the kiss within the context of friendship are likely inspired by Bernard of Clairvaux's allegorical exegesis of the Song of Songs in his fourth sermon on the biblical poem. He compares the "the kiss of the mouth" to the kiss of the feet and the kiss of the hand. These three kisses represent the stages of spiritual growth from repentance and conversion (the kiss of the feet) to moral development (the kiss of the hand) and eventually to the joyous rapture of mystical union (the kiss of the mouth). Bernard of Clairvaux, *Song of Songs* Sermon 4.
7. See Seneca's *Letter to Luciluis*, 9:1; trans. R. M. Gummere, *The Epistles of Seneca*. Vol 1, Loeb Classical Series, vol 4 (New York: Putnam, 1925), 43.
8. 2 Samuel 16:15 – 17:5. Although Hushai is not the most well-known character within the biblical story of King David, Aelred may have felt a special affinity with him since Aelred also served a king by the same name. Aelred's time as the head steward of the Scottish royal household of King David may explain the relatively frequent references to the biblical king throughout *Spiritual Friendship*.

BOOK III

AELRED

So, what brings you here today, Gratian?

GRATIAN

Surely, you know already, Father.

AELRED

Well, yes, I suppose I do, but where is Walter?

GRATIAN

Apparently the one who accused me
of being tardy is now running late.

AELRED

Well, shall we continue the conversation
that we began yesterday?

GRATIAN

Honestly, I'd prefer that we wait for Walter.
He helps me to follow the flow of our conversation
since his knowledge and understanding
honestly exceed my own.

Walter enters.

AELRED

Ho! Walter, did you hear that?
Apparently, Gratian admires you
as a wise friend more than you thought!

WALTER

Perhaps, but Gratian seems to admire everyone.
I think I would have to be exceptionally dull
to not receive his accolades.
But now that we're all here,
let's take advantage of this free time
and pick up where we left off, shall we?

AELRED

Sure. Where were we?
Perhaps we should return to the source
and fountain of all friendship, which is love.
We can love those who are not our friends,
but we cannot be friends
with those whom we do not love.
Sometimes that love bubbles up spontaneously
from our affection and other times
the love grows more intentionally from our will.

Which of these loves, do you think,

is most amenable to spiritual friendship?
Love from affection or love from the will?

WALTER
Well, instead of choosing one or the other,
I would say *both*.
A love that emerges from the affection *and* the will.

AELRED
Excellent answer.

WALTER
But does this mean that everyone
whom I love with my affection and my will
ought to be my spiritual friend?

AELRED
No, not everyone whom you love
ought to be welcomed into the bosom
of spiritual friendship.
A spiritual friend is one to whom
you entrust yourself wholly,
hiding nothing and fearing nothing.
It is only after selecting someone,
exploring their qualities,
and then welcoming them into friendship
that we can enjoy that *special harmony*
of shared interest coupled
with goodwill and affection.

WALTER
Oh, there's that definition of friendship
again which you discussed with Ivo.

Now does that definition apply to *all* friendships?

AELRED
It is a helpful definition for friendship in general;
however, as I said yesterday,
true friendship cannot exist except among the good;
that is, among those who are seeking
to live a good and godly life.

So, we might say spiritual friendship is
a *special harmony of shared interest*
coupled with goodwill and affection
among individuals seeking the good.

GRATIAN
Wonderful! I really like this idea
of friendship as a harmony of shared interest.

WALTER
I like it too, and I especially appreciate
the longer definition for the sake of Gratian,
who seems inclined to sometimes
welcome others into friendship who are
not necessarily seeking to live a good and godly life.

So, how do we discern whether
someone is genuinely seeking the good?
You mentioned selecting, exploring, and then welcoming...

AELRED
Yes, let's start with selecting friends.
First, we generally want to avoid cultivating friendships
with those who are dishonest or arrogant

or untrustworthy or gossipy or easily angered
or some combination of all these.
For instance, if someone has a short fuse,
they will likely explode with anger against a friend,
which is why King Solomon said,
"Do not make friends with hotheads."[1]

GRATIAN
Father, we have both seen you devote
significant time and energy to your friendship
with a very irascible person, who has exploded
with anger in ways that we think are frankly offensive.
In fact, we both saw him do this just a few days ago
and we could tell that you were upset.
How do we reconcile this with what you just said?

WALTER
I was wondering the same thing
but did not have the audacity to speak up about it
since I know how much you care about this person.
(I can always leave it to Gratian to say aloud
what everyone else is thinking.)

AELRED
You are right, Walter,
I do indeed care deeply about this person;
and Gratian, you are also right;
he *is* easily angered, but not so
in the context of our friendship.

GRATIAN
What does *that* mean?
Not so in the context of your friendship?

AELRED

Have you ever seen angry disputes explode between us?

GRATIAN

No, but we imagine this is because
of your patience, not his.

AELRED

That's where you are mistaken.
First, patience is not always the most effective response
to someone's explosive outbursts of anger.
In fact, patient silence often makes the person
even more angry since they may feel
like they are being ignored or silently judged.

Second, this friend of mine respects our friendship
to such an extent that I can curb an outburst now
merely by nodding my head in his direction.
In that simple nod, he knows
that I acknowledge his anger and frustration.

He also knows that the emotions are currently too hot
for any helpful or productive conversation to take place.
In that simple nod, there is an invitation for us both
to cool down and to perhaps release
some anger and tension by praying aloud
some of the more heated Psalms of Lament,
written by the master of spiritual friendship himself:
King David.

After he and I both cool off,
we meet in private to share what's on each other's minds.
We both do this out of respect for our friendship.

I will admit that I am most often the one
who invites him to cool down,
but there have also been times
when he helps me cool down as well.

WALTER
Speaking of cooling down, I think it's time
for Gratian to take a break from interrogating you
about your own personal relationships.

I'd like to know what we should do
if the friends whom we already have in our lives
demonstrate these vices that you mentioned:
dishonesty, arrogance, short temper, and...
forgive me, I'm forgetting the others.
Do we remain friends with them,
or do we dissolve the relationship?

AELRED
These are the vices that we should be looking out for
when it comes to selecting and exploring
the qualities of new friends.

If our current friends exhibit such vices
or develop a habit of doing so, we should first
do whatever we can to help liberate them from these habits.
If that doesn't work, then it's probably time
to discontinue the friendship, but I don't recommend
terminating the relationship abruptly.

Rather, I recommend gradually
unstitching the friendship, little by little.
In the process of unstitching a friendship

with someone who remains addicted to their vices,
be prepared for them to react
by using their vices against you.
For instance, they may spread lies about you to others,
blaming you for their own faults.
Insofar as these insults are tolerable,
endure them out of respect for the friendship
that you once shared.

Although you may need to withdraw your friendship,
never withdraw your love.
And never betray their secrets,
even if they betray yours.
And if they hurt or offend you,
persist in loving them
by continuing to wish for their good.

WALTER
Remind me again of all the vices you mentioned
that would compel us to dissolve
or "unstitch" a friendship in the first place?

AELRED
I mentioned dishonesty, arrogance,
untrustworthiness, gossip, and a short temper.

If any of these seeps into your friendship,
you can become especially vulnerable
to heartache and betrayal;
and to the high probability of your supposed "friend"
revealing your personal secrets to others
or, even worse, using them against you.

To these five, I would add a sixth,
which is not only a major red flag, but a sign
that you need to terminate the friendship right away.

If they have harmed someone
whom you are bound to love and care for
and then persist in doing so
even after you call them to task,
then it is past time for unstitching
that relationship little by little.
Then it is time to liberate yourself
and your loved ones
from the danger as soon as possible.

Remember the Persian king in the Book of Esther.
More than all his other friends,
the Persian king cherished Haman,
but when Haman's deceitful arrogance
threatened the safety of his people
and his beloved wife Esther,
the king had to have the friendship impaled.[2]

GRATIAN
When a friendship is, as you say, "impaled"
for these reasons, it makes me wonder
if it was ever a real friendship in the first place
or if it was just an unhealthy relationship
doomed from the start.

AELRED
Gratian, your wondering leads me
to a very important point that must not be overlooked.
Just because a friendship is dissolved

does not mean that the friendship was completely evil
and rotten from the beginning.
The moments of joyful harmony shared between friends
(even between the Persian King and Haman!)
remain sacred signs and shadows
of a perfectly fulfilled spiritual friendship,
in which no bitterness can ever arise.

WALTER
But wasn't it St. Jerome who said,
"Friendship which can end was never true friendship"?[3]

AELRED
Yes, he did, but what he means is that
a friendship that ends is simply one that failed
to reach the level of a perfectly fulfilled spiritual
friendship.
It does not negate the power of those moments
of special harmony between friends
which point to the eternally true friendship.

It is precisely out of honor
for that true spiritual friendship
that we continue to love
and wish the good for those people
with whom we previously enjoyed that special harmony,
even if such former friends persist in dishonoring us.

WALTER
Now I wonder, if we continue to love
and wish the good for those former friends,
then is the friendship really dissolved
or does the friendship persist?

AELRED
As I said previously,
although there is no friendship without love,
there can still be love without friendship.

A friendship that is on its way to becoming
an eternally true spiritual friendship
is one that includes love (of course),
but also appropriate displays of affection,
emotional security, and opportunities for deep sharing.

If someone has disclosed your personal secrets
to others, then the emotional security
and opportunities for deep sharing are no longer there.
You would not feel emotionally safe
sharing your deep joys and sorrows
and personal secrets with that person.

So, therefore, I would say that
the relationship is no longer a friendship.

WALTER
I see. That makes sense.

GRATIAN
And that's exactly why dishonesty,
untrustworthiness, and gossip are vices for us to avoid
in the process of selecting friends.

AELRED
Yes, if our discussion of this first step
has been sufficient for you,
then I suggest we move on to the next step,

which involves exploring
the qualities and values of a potential friend.

WALTER
Yes please, let's proceed!
My eyes have been glued to the door,
hoping that no one barges in to interrupt
this rich and invigorating conversation.

GRATIAN
I hear the cellarer coming;
and if we let him in,
I'm afraid we won't be able to continue at all.
But look, I'll guard the door!
Please, father, proceed.

AELRED
In exploring someone's qualities and values,
you want to be on the lookout for these four virtues:
loyalty, patience, good intention, and discretion.

WALTER
Loyalty, patience, good intention, and discretion.
OK. Why these four?

AELRED
Let's start with loyalty,
which is perhaps the most praiseworthy virtue of them all.
In our spiritual lives, we are bound to face change.
Friends who are committed to spiritual growth,
both yours and their own, will remain loyal to you
as you face the inevitable changes and chances of this life
that nudge you deeper into radical transformation.[4]

Such friends will also help you practice loyalty
to your own commitments amidst such challenges.[5]

Then there is patience.
Your spiritual journey, I'm sorry to say,
will also include seasons of suffering.

A patient friend will be your lifeline
as you move through such stormy seasons.
They will listen lovingly to you when your heart laments;
and they will also show you how your impatience
can make suffering excessively worse.

When it comes to good intention...
there are also inevitable joys and innumerable gifts
in store for those committed to the spiritual life.
A friend with good intentions will not poach your joy
nor be moved by the possibility of selfish gain
since they have no purpose in the friendship
save the friendship itself and your growth
together in the joy of the Lord.[6]

Finally, discretion.
Your growth in the spiritual life will come
to a grinding halt if you fail to find ways
to share your gifts appropriately with others
through loving service.
A friend with discretion will help guide you
along this road, showing you where
the hungers of the world meet
the great gladness of your heart.[7]

GRATIAN

So, a spiritual friend is loyal while facing change,
patient through seasons of suffering,
well-intentioned amid joyful abundance,
and discerning for loving service.
I understand now why these are the qualities
to seek in a friend, but how do we find and test them?
Must we wait until we are facing major change
or enduring a season of suffering before we can
discover someone's loyalty or patience?

AELRED

Although a friend's faithfulness
is proved best during such difficult seasons,
there are other ways to discern these qualities.
As I said earlier, when a friend betrays your confidence
by disclosing personal secrets,
they have dealt a deathblow to the friendship.

So, following the logic of Jesus, who said,
"those who are faithful in little
will also be faithful in much,"[8]
we would be wise to first confide
only innocuous secrets to these friends.
If the secrets are revealed publicly,
you know they cannot be trusted,
but no real harm will have been done
since the secrets were of little consequence.

On the other hand, if they are found faithful,
then you can begin to share with them
your deeper, more personal secrets. Also,
if they happen to hear false rumors about you,

notice how they respond. If they reject
such malicious tales as nonsense,
then you know that they not only have
the quality of loyalty, but also discretion.

GRATIAN

Yes, I remember hearing about
one of your friends across the sea
responding to malicious rumors about you in just this way.
So that must've been when you knew
he had the qualities of loyalty and discretion!
What about good intention?
How do we know when a friend has good intentions?

AELRED

Notice how they treat the poor
and how they interact with those from whom
they have nothing material or political to gain.
Also, pay attention to how they behave around the wealthy.
If they ignore the poor and fawn over the wealthy,
then beware. They are most likely interested
in you as an asset and not so much as a friend.
If they show genuine generosity to the poor,
then you can likely trust that their intentions
towards you will be good and wholesome.

WALTER

This honestly makes me wonder how much
I may have ignored the poor and tried to flatter the rich.
It also makes me wonder how I may have seen
some of my friendships as opportunities for selfish gain.

AELRED
Because of the world in which we live,
we are conditioned to monetize everything,
even our relationships.
This mindset makes us treat our friends like livestock,
measuring them according to the benefits
they accumulate for us.

These worldly friendships so easily succumb
to the poison of envy, and they will prove toxic
to our own spiritual health and wellbeing.

Spiritual friends, on the other hand,
propel us deeper into the love
that our Savior preached and embodied.
Spiritual friends expand our sense of self,
and, in that ever-widening circle of self-love,
we enfold them![9]

We let them be a mirror reflecting to us
our own belovedness as we offer
that same mirror back to them.
And in beholding this mirror of belovedness,
we come to know friendship as pure gift,
not transaction.

GRATIAN
Thank you, Father,
for teaching us how to recognize, in our friends,
loyalty by watching how they safeguard our secrets,
discretion as they respond to false rumors,
and intentions by observing their interactions with the poor.
Now will you please tell us how we can best identify

patience among those whom we hope to be our friends?

WALTER
Patience is a virtue indeed
and one that Gratian appears to be lacking
in his eagerness to learn more about it.

AELRED
We will inevitably disappoint
and be disappointed by our friends,
which is why patience is so necessary.

One way to explore a friend's patience
is by noticing how they respond to us
when we gently and honestly let them know
how their behavior has disappointed us.

If they initially respond with defensive anger,
then they might not be overflowing with patience.
However, sometimes we ourselves need to be patient
enough with them to let their forbearance bloom.

Patience involves a willingness to feel
whatever we are feeling in the moment,
without judgment, and to trust
that the feelings will eventually pass.

We can trust that our friend's feelings
of defensive anger will eventually pass
so that an honest and loving conversation can later
ensue.
If our friend refuses to ever have such a conversation,
then they lack sufficient patience for true friendship.

GRATIAN

Speaking of an honest conversation,
I need to be honest and admit that this process
of selecting friends and exploring their qualities
seems like an enormous amount of work.
It's almost as if we are putting our
potential friends on probation
while we test their loyalty, discretion,
intention, and patience.

AELRED

Perhaps it is a lot of work,
but the process will prove spiritually formative
for you and for them, and the fruit
of your labor will not only be medicine for your heart
but also sustenance for your soul.

Just consider all the time and effort
we put into choosing sheep and goats, oxen and asses.
How much more attention ought we give
to selecting our friends!

WALTER

I'm afraid I'm starting to agree with Gratian.
It honestly seems easier and safer
to just live without friends altogether.

AELRED

Please understand, Walter.
No one can be happy
without friends.

WALTER
And why not?

AELRED
In the Garden of Eden,
Adam had paradise all to himself,
but God saw that it was not good,
because Adam did not have a suitable friend.
Just imagine having all the riches in the world
but no one to share them with.
Imagine having all the world just to yourself.
Would you be happy?

WALTER
No, I guess not.
I guess I would get lonely.

AELRED
Of course you would,
because the real paradise we seek
is the joy of true friendship,
when we can experience our friend's happiness
as if it were our own.

True friendship is what makes life worth living;
it is a foretaste of heaven on earth.
However, while we are on earth,
friendship takes time and care and even some work.
Aristotle said, "Wanting friends is easy,
but friendship itself is a slow ripening fruit."

The selection and "probation" of our friends
is necessary because not everyone here

is seeking to live a good and godly life
and true spiritual friendship is only possible
among those seeking the good.
In the next life, there will be no need
for probation since we will all be fully ripened
by the sweet goodness of our heavenly Father.

WALTER
Friendship as a foretaste of heaven!
That's really beautiful.

AELRED
It is indeed.
Allow me to explain what I mean
by that with a personal example.
The day before yesterday,
as I was sauntering through
the cloister of the monastery,
I saw our brothers sitting together
in a circle on the lawn.

From an angel's perspective,
they must have looked like a crown of love.
As I looked at them, I became overwhelmed
by my love for each of them as well as their love for me.
Affection coursed through my heart and body.

This love filled me with such joy
that it colored my view of everything around me.
Each blade of grass began to surge with vivacious light,
as if the grass itself was loving me too.
Then when the leaves and branches
of our Rye Valley trees rustled, I heard them sing

the most harmonious song that filled me
with growing gladness and honeyed jubilee
as if I were walking through the
fragrant bowers of Paradise.[10]

I could not help but sing with the psalmist,
"Behold, how good and pleasant it is for brothers—
including brother flower and sister tree!—
to dwell together in unity."[11]
Without friends, even paradise becomes dull,
but when we are with friends,
we can see paradise everywhere.

WALTER
Are you saying
that everyone you saw that day
was your friend?

GRATIAN
Even the grass and the trees?

AELRED
Good questions.
Although I enjoyed a special harmony
with all of them coupled with goodwill and affection,
I would not consider them all spiritual friends
since I do not confide my personal secrets to each of
them.

We may share our secrets with the trees
and even experience with them a friendship of sorts,
but trees cannot share their secrets with us,
at least not in the same way.

When our Lord said to his disciples,
"I no longer call you servants, but friends,"
he explained the reason:
"because I have shared with you
everything I learned from my Father."[12]

St. Ambrose sees in these words
yet another key characteristic of spiritual friendship:
the sharing of our inner hearts.
With spiritual friends, we can lay bare our souls
just as the Lord Jesus poured forth
the mysteries of the Father.
We, of course, would not want to lay bare our souls
to those who lack loyalty, discretion,
patience, or good intention.
So, this leads us to clarify our definition
of spiritual friendship even further.

Spiritual friendship is
a *special harmony of shared interest*
coupled with goodwill and affection
among individuals who can
safely confide in each other
while seeking the good.

WALTER
This spiritual friendship seems so high and lofty
that I feel unable to attain it.
Gratian and I feel more suited for
the kind of friendship that St. Augustine enjoyed
before his conversion,
which he described in his *Confessions*:

A friendship full of laughter,
in which individuals hang out and shoot the breeze,
make each other smile, joke and tease,
read and discuss excellent books together,
delight sometimes in nonsense,
disagreeing occasionally but never bitterly;
a friendship that makes one out of many
through countless small gestures of kindness and play.[13]

AELRED
I would consider this kind of friendship
a carnal friendship, but a beautiful one.

I remember when I spoke with Ivo,
I described carnal friendships as those
that thrive on an unhealthy harmony of violence and vice,
but now I'm inclined to modify my understanding
and to see them as playful and important friendships,
full of potential for spiritual growth.

Carnal friends delight together
in the tangible blessings of this life
and although this could lead to violence and vice,
it does not always have to;
it may also lead to the heavenly blessings
of spiritual friendship.

Worldly friendships, on the other hand,
tend to be doomed from the start
since they are corrupted from the outset
by the pursuit for selfish gain.

As long as the playful mischief

among carnal friends does not hurt anyone,
such friendships should be tolerated and even celebrated
as containing seeds for something higher and holier.

GRATIAN
I'm glad to learn that these beautiful kinds
of carnal friendships contain the seeds
for spiritual friendship.
Even though Walter and I feel a bit too spiritually juvenile
for the sublime friendship you are describing,
I'm wondering how we can water those seeds
of spiritual friendship within our current relationships.

AELRED
Yes, such cultivation of friendship is necessary
not only among those seeking to grow
from carnal to spiritual friendship, but also
for those who already enjoy its goodness.

The key ingredients for cultivating spiritual friendship
are not unlike those values we sought
when exploring potential friends in the first place:
Loyalty remains foundational
for all spiritual friendships, followed by
well-intended and yet frank honesty,
a compassionate and yet discerning heart, and also,
a patient and yet determined perseverance.

Cultivate these virtues within your friendships
and learn to counteract the sinking suspicion
that your friends do not love you
and that they intend to hurt you.
This suspicion will poison you and your relationship.

Relax into the levity and ease of friendship,
trusting that they are wishing for your good.

Trust also that I am praying for your ultimate good
on a regular basis, asking that you be held
by God's providence, guided by God's purpose,
and filled with God's peace.[14]

GRATIAN
Wow! Thank you.
I feel so honored to be on the receiving end
of your prayers, my superior.

AELRED
One important law of friendship is that
a superior must be on an equal plane with an inferior.
We are to let the lofty descend and the lowly rise,
the rich become poor and the poor rich,
on the equal playing field of friendship.

King Saul's son, Prince Jonathan,
demonstrated this marvelously
in his friendship with David.
Prince Jonathan did not let his royal status
get in the way of his friendship.
Even when his father Saul
tried to arouse envy between the two
by reminding Jonathan that David was going
to dishonor him and strip him of his kingdom,
Jonathan remained a loyal, well-intentioned,
discerning, and patient friend.

Jonathan knew that without friends,

even paradise (or an entire kingdom) would become dull,
but with David as his friend,
he could see paradise everywhere.

Jonathan loved his friend so much
that he was even ready to hand over
his regal power to him, saying,
"You shall be king, and I will be next after you."[15]

Cicero honestly would have been shocked
by Jonathan's generosity since he could not
imagine anyone sincerely preferring
the honor of a friend over their own,
but thanks to Jonathan, we have an example
of a true, perfect, constant, and eternal friendship,
uncorrupted by envy and undiminished by suspicion.[16]
Seek to be a friend to someone in the same way
that Jonathan was a friend to David.

WALTER
It is one thing for Jonathan
to abdicate the throne for the sake of friendship,
but another thing entirely for him to then
give the throne to his friend.
That honestly seems extreme to me.
I feel like that would be as extreme
as you handing over your abbacy to Gratian![17]

AELRED
Yes, if it seems too difficult or impossible
for us to follow Jonathan's example, then
let's at least seek to be on equal footing with our
friends.

When we strive towards equality in friendship,
we need to be ready to relinquish money, land, or power.
If we ever hope to be of one heart
and one soul with our friends,
then we should also not hesitate to be of one purse.
For where our treasure is, there our heart will be also.[18]
And if we give money or goods to a friend,
let us never do so condescendingly,
but cheerfully in a way that preserves their dignity.
Remember when Boaz saw Ruth
collecting ears of corn behind his reapers.
He ordered his reapers to leave extra for her
in such a way that did not shame her.[19]
May we also anticipate the needs of our friends
and meet their needs lovingly,
almost as if they were doing *us* a favor.

WALTER
But, Father, we live in a monastery,
where we receive no money or goods
and therefore having nothing to give away.
How do you expect us to follow these teachings?

AELRED
A wise man once said that
most of our problems would be solved
if we simply removed the words
"mine" and "yours" from our lexicon.

In the monastery, we are mostly free
from the selfish greed that so often
becomes a nasty pest among friends.
Holy poverty, which we enjoy,

safeguards our friendships.
When you consider all the resources
of spiritual love available to you,
you have so much to give away.

You can give generously of your empathy,
care, and compassion.
You can rejoice with your friends
when they are elated
and grieve with them when they are sad,
regarding their ups and downs as your own.

You can bless them with what Cicero called
the greatest adornment of friendship:
reverential respect.[20]
And one way you can show them such respect
is by speaking words of truth to them,
especially if they need some gentle admonishment.
Remember the words of wise King Solomon who said,
"Wounds inflicted by a friend
are more appreciated
than kisses from a flatterer."[21]

However, when it comes to both
praising and admonishing your friends,
always practice moderation.
In fact, preserve moderation in all things,
except perhaps in prayer.
You can never be too generous
with your prayers for your friends.
Your prayer for their ultimate good
should be echoing especially powerfully
in your heart whenever you offer

words of admonishment so that
the words are offered and received
with genuine love, affection, and affirmation.

GRATIAN
I appreciate what you're suggesting
because I know several people
who are usually too afraid to offer
any words of admonishment
because they don't want to hurt their friend's feelings.
I'll admit that I might be one of those people myself.

WALTER
Yes, and I know several people
who seem to get some weird pleasure
out of admonishing their friends, even publicly.
I sure hope I'm *not* one of those people.

AELRED
Your willingness to potentially see yourself
among the often-maligned community
known as "those people" is admirable.
Offering words of genuine admonishment
with gentle compassion is a skill
that takes prudence and practice and mostly prayer.

Remember how the Prophet Nathan
offered words of genuine admonishment
to David when the king yielded to lust
and then added murder to adultery.
Out of respect for his royal majesty,
the prophet did not accuse him
bluntly nor aggressively.

We can even imagine the prophet
praying for the king's ultimate good
when he prudently told the truth to the king
through the slant of a powerful parable.[22]

GRATIAN
Yes, I'm frankly surprised that King David
did not have the prophet Nathan beheaded
or at least demoted for calling him out
as the guilty man in the parable
whom King David believed to be worthy of execution.

WALTER
Yes, David and Nathan must have had
a solid spiritual friendship, strong enough
to hold the heat of that conversation...
And now that you got me thinking
about the friendship between David and Nathan
and reflecting on the king's power
to either promote or demote the prophet,
I'm wondering what you think, Father,
about the role of friendship in
promoting people to positions of authority.

For instance, when you promote people to offices,
do you tend to choose from among your closest friends
or do you use some different criteria?

AELRED
I certainly do not promote people
to offices of authority merely because
they are among my friends. In the process
of appointing people to office,

I seek to be guided by reason, not affection.

Unfortunately, some of my friends
have felt unloved by me simply because
I did not promote them to certain positions,
when in fact, my decision to not promote them
was an act of love and compassion.

I really do not think of such roles and positions
as gifts for me to bestow on friends; rather,
I think of them as significant responsibilities
that others are called to carry.

So, in discerning that call, I ask myself,
"Will this responsibility be too heavy of a burden
for this person to endure?"
If so, then I seek someone else
for whom the burden is more manageable
and perhaps even pleasurable.

Once again, we can turn to Scripture
for an example of this.
Jesus himself promoted Peter
as the leader of the church,
giving him the keys to the kingdom.
So, does this mean that he loved Peter more than John?

Not at all.
John was perhaps Jesus's dearest friend,
known as the disciple whom he loved,
the friend to whom he commended his mother,
the friend to whom he revealed the secrets of his heart;
indeed, John was the friend who leaned

on the bosom of his master and listened to his heartbeat.
John did not seek this intimacy with Jesus
to receive promotions or vain honors.
No, the goal of the intimacy was the intimacy itself.[23]

GRATIAN
Father, I appreciate all these examples of friendship
that you provide from Scripture.
However, since you also teach us to discover
the teachings of the Spirit in our own experience,
I wonder if you can share a personal experience
about your own friendships.[24]

AELRED
Absolutely. In fact, I was just remembering
two close friends who are no longer living,
but who remain very much alive in my heart.
They both began as companions
with whom I shared *a special harmony of shared interest*,
specifically in our common love for the monastic life.[25]

I met the first friend when I was young,
and our shared interest was *coupled with much affection*.
As I began to wish good things for him and pray for him,
our companionship evolved into a burgeoning friendship.
I began to explore his qualities and values,
eager to know how genuinely he sought
to live a good and godly life. Sadly,
just as our friendship was beginning to bloom,
he was ripped away from me.[26]

I met the second friend when *he* was young,
and I was able to explore his qualities and values

more thoroughly. When I saw evidence
of his *loyalty, patience, good intentions,* and *discretion,*
I became more and more convinced that
he was seeking to live a good and godly life;
and I felt that I could *safely confide in him.*

We who began as companions became friends
and then the most cherished of friends.
Our friendship was indeed a *special harmony*
of shared interest coupled with goodwill
and affection as we safely confided in each other
while seeking the good.

After consulting the other brothers,
I decided to promote him to the role of subprior,
a position that he initially resisted, claiming
that he was too young and too inexperienced;
but more than anything else,
he was concerned that the
demands and responsibilities
of the position might place
undue stress on our friendship.

Because he shared his honest fears and concerns with me,
our friendship grew even stronger.
He served as a superb subprior and,
throughout his term, we were able
to speak to each other with both frankness and affection.

Eventually, our hearts became so fused together
that he became a refuge for my spirit,
a solace for my grief, a counsel for my confusion,
and refreshment for my soul.

Through this experience of loving and being loved
we were both given a foretaste of Heaven
because the love that flows between spiritual friends
forms wings that flutter and fling us
into the sublime splendor of divine love,
into the very bosom of Christ upon which
the disciple-turned-friend found true rest.

GRATIAN

A truly glorious spiritual friendship!
I must say that the second friend sounds like Ivo,
with whom you began this conversation many years ago.
I just can't remember if he ever served as a subprior...

WALTER

Perhaps there is a good reason, Gratian,
why Father has chosen to withhold his friend's name.[27]

AELRED

It is getting late, my brothers,
and we must at last bring this discussion to a close.
But before we do, allow me to make three final points,
which might be the most important of all.

First, before you can properly love someone else
as a spiritual friend, you must learn to love yourself.[28]
Some monks think they are being holy by hating themselves.
Do not be like them. They are wrong.
We love ourselves by naturally wanting
what is best for ourselves and
one way to cultivate this healthy self-love
is by directing our prayers of goodwill
compassionately to our own hearts

and to those parts of ourselves
we sometimes fail to love.

Second, the reason you want to
choose your friends wisely is because
they can either move you deeper
along the transformative path of love or away from it.
If your friends are loyal, patient,
well-intentioned, and discerning,
then they can help accompany you and guide you
through life's inevitable changes, sufferings,
joys, and opportunities for loving service.

If your friends look upon your friendship as a gift
rather than a transaction, then the mere sound
of your name will bring a smile to their face
and thus offer you a faint glimpse
of God's affection for you.

And if your friends can speak to you
with both frankness and compassion,
then you will experience the same spiritual delight
that inspired the psalmist to sing, "Behold!
How good and pleasant it is for brothers
to dwell together in unity."

Third and finally, pray for one another.
Prayers from a friend are the most effective prayers of all,
especially when they are offered with
tears of love and affection.

So, pray the prayer of goodwill for your friend,
asking for their happiness, their safety,

and their growth in virtue,
pray that God's providence sustains them,
God's purpose guides them,
and God's peace fills them,
because whenever you pray to Christ for a friend,
your love for your friend becomes one
with Christ's love for them;
and sometimes imperceptibly,
through your prayers, this one love
arrives in your friend's life
as a warm and unexpected embrace,
which is the embrace of Christ himself.

And although we might taste this spiritual fruit
best among our friends in this life,
with whom we enjoy that special harmony
of shared interest, do not doubt
that this can also be experienced
with friends who have passed on to the next life
because friendship will always overcome
the sting of death.

And do not hesitate to pray the prayer of goodwill
for all those whom you have, for good reason,
chosen *not* to welcome into
the mystery of friendship in this life.
Pray also for your casual companions
and for those whom you find difficult to love
and even for those who are sinful and greedy
and for those who have hurt you or broke your heart.

Pray for them all,
asking God for their happiness,

safety, peace, and growth along the way,
because in the life to come,
spiritual friendship will be outpoured upon all.
For some, the friendship will feel like
the sun and for others it will feel like the rain.
God will outpour his friendship upon all;
and all will outpour their friendship upon God,
who is the Source of all Friendship
and the One who, in the end, shall be all in all.

---

1. Proverbs 22:24.
2. Esther 7:9.
3. Jerome, Epistle 3:6.
4. The phrase "changes and chances" is culled from the following prayer: "Be present, O merciful God, and protect us...so that we who are wearied by the changes and chances of this life may rest in your eternal changelessness; through Jesus Christ our Lord." The Episcopal Church. The Book of Common Prayer, 133.
5. In his book *Spiritual Friendship after Religion: Walking with People while the Rules Are Changing,* Joseph A. Stewart-Sicking reflects on Aelred's four qualities of loyalty, patience, good intention, and discretion within the context of Alexander John Shaia's four-path journey of change, suffering, joy, and service. The four-path journey known as Quadratos correlates with the Four Gospels and, in this distillation, Aelred explicitly correlates the four qualities with the four paths, a connection that is not explicit but arguably implicit in the original text. See Joseph A. Stewart-Sicking, *Spiritual Friendship after Religion: Walking with People while the Rules Are Changing* (New York: Morehouse Publishing, 2016); Alexander John Shaia with Michelle L. Gaugy, *Heart and Mind: The Four-Gospel Journey for Radical Transformation* (Preston Australia: Mosaic Press, 2013).
6. In *The Prophet,* Kahlil Gibran writes, "Let there be no purpose in friendship save the deepening of the spirit." Kahlil Gibran, *The Prophet* (New York: Alfred A. Knopf, 1966), 59.
7. "The place God calls you," according to theologian and author Frederick Buechner, "is where your deep gladness and the world's deep hunger meet." Frederick Buechner, *Wishful Thinking: A Seeker's ABC* (New York: HarperOne, 1993), 118-119.
8. Luke 16:10.

9. The Austrian poet Rainer Maria Rilke wrote, "I live my life in ever-widening circles that reach out across the world." Rainer Maria Rilke, *Rilke's Book of Hours: Love Poems to God*, trans. Anita Barrows and Joanna Macy (New York: Riverhead Books, 2005), 45.

10. The literary character Walter in *Spiritual Friendship* likely represents the actual Walter Daniel, who wrote *The Life of Aelred*, in which he beautifully describes the music of the trees at Rievaulx: "When the branches of lovely trees clash and part with a rhythmical soughing as the leaves flutter gently to the ground, the blissful listener enjoys a wealth of jubilant harmony and his receptive ears are charmed by so sweet a blending of tumultuous sound, where each of the myriad different notes is yet musically equal to the rest." Walter Daniel, *Life of St. Aelred* 5; *The Cistercian World: Monastic Writings of the Twelfth Century*, trans. Pauline Matarasso (New York: Penguin Books, 1993), 154.

11. Psalm 133:1. This same verse is quoted in John Cassian's brief description of spiritual friendship in his *Conferences*. 16.13.

12. John 15:15.

13. Augustine, *Confessions* 4.8.13.

14. In Aelred's *Pastoral Prayer*, we can read the prayers that Aelred prayed for his monks and friends. *Aelred of Rievaulx: Treatises & Pastoral Prayer*, 103 – 118.

15. 1 Samuel 23:17.

16. Cicero, *De Amicitia*, 17.63.

17. Aelred certainly did not hand over the Rievaulx abbacy to Gratian. Aelred's successor was Silvanus who served as abbot from 1167 to 1188.

18. Matthew 6:21.

19. Ruth 2:15 – 16.

20. Cicero, *De Amicitia*, 22.82.

21. Proverbs 27:6.

22. 2 Samuel 12:1.

23. In *A Rule of Life for a Recluse*, Aelred offers a threefold meditation that invites reflection on the past, present, and future events of our salvation. In meditating on the past, he invites his sister, a recluse, to imagine herself present during the events of Christ's life, including the Last Supper. He writes, "Why are you in such a hurry to go out now? Wait a little while. Do you see? Who is that, I ask, who is reclining on his breast and bends back his head to lay it in his bosom? Happy is he, whoever he may be. O, I see: his name is John. O John, tell us what sweetness, what grace and tenderness, what light and devotion you are imbibing from that fountain. There indeed are all the treasures of wisdom and knowledge, the fountain of mercy, the abode of loving kindness, the honeycomb of eternal sweetness. What have you done to deserve all this, John? Are you higher than Peter, more holy than Andrew, and more pleasing than all the

other apostles?" *Treatises & Pastoral Prayer,* trans. Theodore Berkeley OCSO, 86 – 87.

24. "You are able to study the hidden things of the spirt not so much in books as in your own experience." Aelred of Rievaulx, *Jesus at the Age of Twelve* 19 (p. 25). St. Bernard begins his third sermon on the Song of Songs, saying, "Today we read the book of experience." Bernard of Clairvaux, *Song of Songs* Sermon 3.

25. C. S. Lewis explains that friendship arises from companionship, which he calls "the matrix of Friendship," explaining, "many people when they speak of their 'friends' mean only their companions. But it is not Friendship...By saying this I do not at all intend to disparage the merely Clubbable relation. We do not disparage silver by distinguishing it from gold." Today we might compare Lewis's "Clubbable relation" to colleagues or "Facebook friends." Lewis continues, "It may be a common religion, common studies, a common profession, even a common recreation. All who share it will be our companions; but one or two or three who share something more will be our Friends." C. S. Lewis, *The Four Loves,* 96 – 97.

26. This friend is usually identified as Simon, whom Aelred writes about in *The Mirror of Charity*: "The recent death of my dear Simon forcibly drives me...to weep for him." Aelred of Rievaulx, *The Mirror of Charity,* trans. Elizabeth Connor OCSO (Kalamazoo MI: Cistercian Publications, 1990), Book I. 34 (p. 147).

27. F. M. Powicke identifies this second friend as Geoffrey of Dinant, not Ivo. See F. M. Powicke, *Aelred of Rievaulx and his Biographer Walter Daniel* (Manchester: Longmans Green and Co., 1922), 50.

28. "You can never love another person unless you are equally involved in the beautiful, but difficult, spiritual work of learning to love yourself." John O'Donohue, *Anam Cara,* 50.

APPENDIX

SPIRITUAL PRACTICE 1
AELREDIAN PRAYER OF GOODWILL

J ust as Aelred was inspired by a non-Christian authority, Cicero, to employ the format of dialogue in offering his meditation on spiritual friendship, so too have I been inspired by a non-Christian tradition, Buddhism, to employ the format of *Mettā* in offering a meditation on Aelred's spiritual friendship. *Mettā*, which is Pali for "loving-kindness," is a Buddhist meditation practice that I have used in classroom and retreat settings to help embody the teachings of Aelred, whose emphasis on goodwill (i.e., wishing the good for our friends) and the ever-widening circles of self-love resonate deeply with this practice. Participants have always appreciated the loving energy that the practice engenders.

Use the following prompts or variations of them to experience and/or guide others through this Aelredian Prayer of Goodwill practice.[1] Do not move too quickly through the prompts but try to linger with each invitation.

Begin by getting into a position
in which you feel comfortable and alert.
So, start by taking care of yourself.

...Now bring to mind a friend
whom you love and who you know loves you,
A friend who is easy to love.

Don't overthink the friend or the friendship.
Keep it simple.
Bring this friend to mind.
The friend can be a family member or partner.
Bring that friend here.
See the friend looking at you with love and joy.
And just enjoy your love for one another.
Soak it in, breathe it in, taste it and drink it.
Relax into it.

"A great blessing of friendship," Aelred says,
"is the freedom from anxiety with which
you entrust and commit yourself to a friend."[2]
Aelred quotes Ambrose, who says,
"Let the graces of each friend blend with the other."[3]
Let your graces blend with each other.
Relax into the love and the quality of the friendship.
Feel the love, affection, reassurance,
and joy of your friendship.

Now offer a prayer for your friend.
You can pray whatever you want.
Or you can pray the following simple prayer
(or customize it):

76

May you be happy.
May you be safe.
May you be at peace.

Aelred concludes his reflection on spiritual friendship
with these words: "Finally, pray for one another.
Prayers from a friend are the most effective prayers of all,
especially when they are offered
with tears of love and affection...

"So, pray the prayer of goodwill for your friend,
asking for their happiness, their safety,
and their growth in virtue, pray that
God's providence sustains them,
God's purpose guides them,
and God's peace fills them."

Praying for your friend,
May you be happy.
May you be safe.
May you be at peace.

Now direct your prayerful attention
and love to your inner life.
Look at yourself through the eyes
of the friend who loves you.

Experience yourself as the one loved, the beloved.
Direct the love that you have for your friend
towards yourself and your inner life.

Aelred says, "Before you can properly love someone else
as a spiritual friend, you must learn to love yourself."

Love yourself as your neighbor.
And now offer a prayer for yourself.
You may even want to put your hand
on your heart as you pray:

May you be happy.
May you be safe.
May you be at peace.

Praying again:

May you be happy.
May you be safe.
May you be at peace.

Rest in that love and goodwill for yourself.
Aelred says that loyalty, patience,
good intention, and discretion
are the four qualities to seek and celebrate in a friend.

Rest in the loyalty, patience,
good intention, and discretion
that your friend has for you
and rest in the loyalty, patience, good intention,
and discretion that you have with yourself.

Now widen the circle of that love and friendship...
Widen the circle to include everyone you know,
even those who are irascible,
or annoying, or difficult to love.
Expand your experience of friendship and love
to include everyone around you and everyone you know.

And now praying for everyone you know, pray:

May you be happy.
May you be safe.
May you be at peace.

Aelred says,
"Whenever you pray to Christ for a friend,
your love for your friend becomes one
with Christ's love for them; and sometimes
imperceptibly, through your prayers,
this one love arrives in your friend's life
as a warm and unexpected embrace,
which is the embrace of Christ himself."

Let your affection for your friend melt
into your affection for Christ
and even your affection for yourself
and taste the sweetness of that love.

Finally, with this experience of love,
affection, and friendship in your heart and mind,
listen to these words of Aelred of Rievaulx:

"The day before yesterday,
as I was sauntering through the cloister
of the monastery, I saw our brothers
sitting together in a circle on the lawn.
From an angel's perspective,
they must have looked like a crown of love.

"As I looked at them, I became overwhelmed
by my love for each of them as well as their love for me.

Affection coursed through my heart and body.

"This love filled me with such joy
that it colored my view of everything around me.
Each blade of grass began to surge with vivacious light,
as if the grass itself was loving me too.

"Then when the leaves and branches
of our Rye Valley trees rustled, I heard them
sing the most harmonious song that filled me
with growing gladness and honeyed jubilee
as if I were walking through the fragrant bowers
of Paradise.

"I could not help but sing with the psalmist,
'Behold, how good and pleasant it is for brothers
—including brother flower and sister tree!—
to dwell together in unity.'"[4]

---

1. The goal of this practice is to cultivate goodwill, *benevolentia*. Adele Fiske writes that for both Ambrose and Aelred, "the source and nature of friendship is not in the intellect...but in the will, *benevolentia*." Adele Fiske, "The Survival and Development of the Ancient Concept of Friendship in the Early Middle Ages." PhD dissertation. Fordham University, 1955, p. 114, as cited in Marsha L. Dutton, "Introduction," *Spiritual Friendship* (Collegeville MN: Liturgical Press, 2010), 28.
2. Aelred of Rievaulx, *Spiritual Friendship*, trans. Lawrence C. Braceland, III.28 (p. 95).
3. Ambrose, *De officiis* 3.133, as cited in Aelred of Rievaulx, *Spiritual Friendship*, trans. Lawrence C. Braceland, III.30 (p. 95).
4. For more information on the Buddhist practice of *Mettā*, see Bhante Henepola Gunaratana, *Loving-Kindness in Plain English: The Practice of Metta* (Somerville MA: Wisdom Publications, 2017).

SIRITUAL PRACTICE 11
WRITE AND SHARE YOUR OWN
THREEFOLD PRAYER

The Aelredian Prayer of Goodwill is anchored in the basic threefold intention of the *Mettā* meditation: *May you be happy. May you be safe. May you be at peace.* In his *Rule of Life for a Recluse*, Aelred invited his sister to practice a threefold meditation;[1] and in his *Pastoral Prayer*, he offered prayers for his friends and for the monks under his care. Below are examples of threefold prayers based on Aelred's *Spiritual Friendship* and *Pastoral Prayer*:

May you be truly happy.
May you be healthy and safe.
May you grow in virtue, love, and grace.

or

May God's gracious providence hold and sustain you.
May God's loving purpose gladden and guide you.
May God's perfect peace fill you now and always.

or more simply

May you be held by God's providence,
led by God's purpose,
and filled with God's peace.

Write your own threefold prayer of goodwill for friends, others, and yourself. As you reflect, consider what it is that you ultimately hope for yourself and consider what prayers you would want someone else to pray for you. Finally, consider how your threefold prayer may or may not resonate with the teachings of Aelred.

When this invitation is offered in a group setting, participants are encouraged to not only share their threefold prayers but to also pray them aloud for everyone else in the group.

---

1. In reference to St. Aelred and other Cistercian fathers, Merton writes, "Three is their favorite number, according to the traditional division of three ways, purgative, illuminative, and unitive." Thomas Merton, *What Are These Wounds?: The Life of a Cistercian Mystic: Saint Lutgarde of Aywières* (Milwaukee WI: Bruce Publishing, 1950), 99.

SPIRITUAL PRACTICE 111
BEFRIENDING A TREE

*S*pend at least 20 minutes sitting under the shade of a tree. *Acknowledge the tree as a sentient being with whom you can have a kind of conversation and whom you might even befriend.*

IN HIS LETTER TO AELRED, Bernard wrote, "My friend, you have discovered things in the woods that you would have never found in books. Stones and trees have taught you things that you would have never learned from your schoolteachers. Your experience of simply sitting under the shade of trees...has given you wisdom that ought to be shared." In another letter to Henry Murdac, an Englishman who later became an abbot and archbishop, St. Bernard wrote, "Woods and stones will teach you what you can never learn from any master." As an Anglican priest who traces his spiritual lineage back to the medieval English Cistercians, I receive these words of Bernard as a special part of my English spiritual heritage. I invite others to claim these words as part of their spiritual heritage as well.

Even if Bernard's nature imagery is interpreted and explained away as biblical symbolism for Cistercian work and contemplation, the invitation still remains for us to reflect on the spiritual wisdom of the tree, which towers perhaps above all other symbols in the biblical canon. [1] The Bible begins and ends with a tree: the tree of life in the Garden of Eden (Genesis 2:9) and the tree of life in the New Jerusalem (Revelation 22:2). A tree also stands in the center of the Bible, in the first Psalm, which functions as an introduction to and summary of the entire Psalter: a tree planted by streams of water (Psalm 1:3).[2] The tree remains dominant in the Christian tradition, which venerates the Holy Cross of Christ as the Tree of Life upon which our Savior died. One of the great Old English poems of the eighth century was called *The Dream of the Rood* which describes the cross as a tree which proceeds to speak to the poet and tell the poet the story of how it was cut down from the edge of the woods and made into a cross. Marie-Madeleine Davy explains that one of the two most popular symbols of the Middle Ages was "the cosmic tree, identified as the tree of life and the cross."[3] Historian Sara Ritchey recounts the story of a fourteenth-century Dominican nun named Alheit of Trochau who rushed from one tree to another in her convent in Germany, embracing the trunks of trees and holding them close to her heart and saying to her sisters, "Each tree is our Lord Jesus Christ."[4]

While some insist that St. Bernard was not a nature mystic, it is worth noting that the earliest account of the saint's life reports him joking merrily among his friends and saying that he had no spiritual teacher other than the oaks and beeches.[5]

Some of the earliest accounts of St. Francis describe him

and his followers frequently wandering and praying in the woods among the trees. I like to think that these trees were not peripheral but rather essential to Francis's story and sainthood. Amos Clifford, the founder of the Association of Nature and Forest Therapy, says something similar about the Buddha. He says, "The more I spend time in the forest, the more I think about, 'What did the Buddha do?' He wandered around in the forest. Where was he sitting at the moment of his enlightenment? He was sitting at the base of a tree. Now I always thought of that in the past as just an interesting setting for the story. But the more I connect with trees and the more I'm in forest environments, the more I begin to suspect that it's actually an essential part of the story, that there's something about the combined sentience of the person and the tree being in relationship that supported the Buddha's awakening."[6] There is indeed something about the combined sentience of a person and a tree that can support *our* spiritual awakening.

According to Jewish philosopher Martin Buber, if we become attentive enough to a tree, we can sense the tree becoming attentive to us. Perhaps we can also sense the presence of God, which permeates all things, infusing the tree and looking back at us.[7]

In John 1:43–51, Nathaniel seems to undergo a mystical experience under the shade of a fig tree. I now wonder if Nathaniel experienced and felt the presence of God in the tree and even felt God looking back at him through the tree. So, when Jesus says to him, "I saw you under the fig tree," Nathaniel has an epiphany about the divine identity of this prophetic rabbi: "You must be the Son of God and the King of Israel, if you were the one who saw me under the tree!" (John 1:49).

Bernard said to his friend Aelred, "Your experience of

simply sitting under the shade of trees...has given you wisdom that ought to be shared."[8] One of the final invitations in a Forest Therapy walk is to sit at the base of a tree and to befriend it. The final invitation in this book on spiritual friendship, which was partly inspired by Bernard's words, is to go and do the same. Share whatever wisdom you received in the process.

---

1. Emero Stiegman, "'Woods and Stones' & 'The Shade of Trees' in the Mysticism of Saint Bernard" in *Truth as Gift: Studies in Honor of John R. Sommerfeldt*, ed. Marsha Dutton et. al. (Kalamazoo MI: Cistercian Publications, 2004), 321–354.

2. The prophet Jeremiah elaborates on this same image when he writes, "Blessed are those who trust in the Lord...they shall be like a tree planted by water, sending out its roots by the stream." (Jeremiah 17:7–8).

3. Marie-Madeleine Davy, *Initation à la Symbolique Romane (XII Siécle), nouvelle edition de l'Essai sur la Symbolique Romane* (Paris: Flammarion, 1977), 213, as cited in Emero Stiegman, "'Woods and Stones' & 'The Shade of Trees' in the Mysticism of Saint Bernard," 352.

4. Sara Ritchey, "Spiritual Arborescence: Trees in the Medieval Christian Imagination" *Spiritus: A Journal of Christian Spirituality* (Johns Hopkins University Press) Vol 8. No. 1. Spring 2008, pp. 64-82.

5. Vita Prima 1.23.

6. Amos Clifford, https://www.ttbook.org/interview/bathing-beauty-trees

7. This deeply orthodox Christian truth is known as pan-entheism: God *in* all things, *not* pantheism (which states that God is all things), but pan-entheism.

8. In his poem "The Tables Turned," Walt Whitman similarly taught, "One impulse from a vernal wood may teach you more of man, of moral evil and of good than all the sages can."

AFTERWORD

Ten years ago, I was ordained to the priesthood at St. John's Episcopal Cathedral in Los Angeles on January 11, the Eve of the Feast Day of St. Aelred of Rievaulx (1110–1167). Although I had previously offered lectures on St. Aelred and Cistercian spirituality in my English spirituality class, I had not yet been gripped by the saint in the same way that I had been gripped by other medieval authors, such as the fourteenth-century English mystics. The fact that my first full day of ordained ministry as a priest—indeed the first day I ever celebrated Eucharist—fell on Aelred's feast day began to claim more of my attention and, as I dived more deeply into his writings, I gradually became more astounded by the modern relevance of his wisdom, especially his emphasis on goodwill for others and the necessity for healthy self-love in friendships. His teachings began to inform my friendships, some of which I may have, at times, taken for granted. His wisdom was inviting me to start practicing a more intentional gratitude, especially when it came to my friends.

Tragically, in the process of writing this distillation, I lost two of my closest spiritual friends to suicide. Although their circumstances were remarkably different, they both made a decision that ripped my heart out of my chest and left me aching daily for their presence. They each wrote letters to me before they died and signed off with similar valedictions: "One Love" and "Eternal Love." While their despair was paramount, their simple words suggested to me that they both had some sense of hope that our love and friendship might somehow endure. Soon Aelred's comments about the persistence of friendship beyond death began to shimmer with more meaning and promise for me. At the beginning of Book II, Aelred says, "Although my beloved Ivo has passed on from this life, he remains very close to me in spirit [because] spiritual friends remain alive even after they have died." My friends both felt very alive to me when I returned to Chartres cathedral, a destination to which I had previously dragged them both during our European backpacking trip when we were in our early 20s. They both felt very alive to me when I rented a car in Leeds after completing my training as a Forest Therapy Guide in Yorkshire and drove to the abbey ruins of Rievaulx to walk among the "bowers of paradise." And I am grateful that my beloved spiritual friends have both felt very alive to me at Our Lady of the Redwoods Abbey, where I have had the joy of praying with Aelred's brothers and sisters, the Cistercian monks, *sub umbris arborum,* under the shade of trees.

Feast of St. John Cassian, 2024
Redwoods Monastery, Whitethorn CA

Made in the USA
Monee, IL
01 September 2024

64943442R00069